T0305027

creative struggle is real

STOP PROCRASTINATING AND START MAKING

HOLLY BLONDIN

BISPUBLISHERS

BIS Publishers
Borneostraat 80-A
1094 CP Amsterdam
The Netherlands
T +31 (0)20 515 02 30
bis@bispublishers.com
www.bispublishers.com

ISBN 978 90 636 9670 2

Cover design by Nihal Pimpale
Book design by Jessica Saggu

This book is dedicated to you, dear reader—
to your growth as a creator, maker, and imaginator,
and your remarkable creative courage.

Without you,
these pages would never come to life.
For an unopened book is as inert as an untapped imagination.

Contents

01 Part 1: Defining your creative context

02 Part 2: Designing your creative practice

03 Part 3:
Maintaining your creative momentum

04 Part 4:
More ways to make

How to use this book

Dive in and start making. Write and draw on the pages. Get messy.

Use the creative challenges and activity spreads throughout the book to activate and strengthen your creative muscles. Follow them in order or choose one at random to explore.

You could also use the exercises with your creative team. Go straight to a challenge and invite everyone to take part and start making. Then share and discuss your creations.

For the deepest creative journey, start from the beginning and work your way through to the end. The three different sections of the book are **designed to build on one another to assist you in developing creative momentum that lasts, one stage at a time.** You'll begin with Part 1, *Defining your creative context*, before moving to Part 2, *Designing your creative practice*, and ending with Part 3, *Maintaining your creative momentum.*

Think of this interactive guidebook as a friendly creative companion, supporting you every step of the way as you embark on your next creative adventure and face the creative struggle.

Introduction

For as long as I can remember, I have been making things. I grew up in a small town in the country with a big yard and a group of neighbourhood kids to play make-believe with. We spent our days making cakes out of mud and then selling them at the "bakery" we designed using lawn furniture and plastic buckets. Some of our best creations came out of the wood scraps my father, a carpenter, would leave behind in his woodshop. We were always looking for creative inspiration in our surroundings.

Like most children, I never questioned the act of making in those days. I just did it. If I had an idea, I would gather the resources closest to me and get creating. If I was moved to tell a story, I would write it down, recite from my favourite children's books, or gather my friends to create a play or a dance we'd share with our parents. Making didn't have barriers. Ideas weren't abstract dreams, or things *other people* did. Making was a way of life. It infused our reality with imagination, and doing it together made us feel seen and accepted.

But even with this early education in making, my creative journey has been less than straightforward.

Let's leave these memories of joyful childhood creation behind and fast-forward a few decades, to my professional life in marketing. What had once been a natural act of making had become a source of pressure. Making without thinking now seemed like a luxury I couldn't afford. My approach to creativity started to be shaped by others people's expectations. I found myself following the rules set by the directors, managers, company visionaries, and brands I worked with. During those years, I became detached from my own artistic capacities and creative voice. I put off making, and exchanged it for waiting, procrastinating, and filling my time with other things. Something was missing, but I didn't know how I'd lost it. And I was struggling with where and how to find it.

I found myself asking the same questions that likely brought you to this book:

What happened to my impulse to create? And how can I get it back?

Whether or not you consider yourself a creative person—and newsflash: the idea of the "non-creative" is a myth!—almost everyone remembers what it felt like to experiment, play, and make as a child. Each and every one of us is creative and capable.

But as we enter formal education and the workforce, many of us lose our ability to connect with our creative resources. We forget how to make.

Our culture values results over process. Rather than thinking about creativity as a practice, we're generally taught to focus on the end result. All too often, I see enormously talented professionals still asking for permission to use their creative capacities, more comfortable with copy-pasting the "right" answers into the frameworks they're familiar with. Even organisations that promote innovation often try to fast-track creativity by demanding immediate results, creating unrealistic expectations, and bypassing the creative process. Add that to our cultural tendency to divide people up into "creatives" and "non-creatives", and it's no wonder that so many of us feel a creative disconnect.

So what can we do about it?

In my case, the path back to creativity came through an unexpected opportunity.

Throughout my MBA and my marketing career, I couldn't shake the sense I wasn't using all of my creative potential. The longing to connect to my personal creativity grew, but I couldn't seem to get back the imaginative rhythm I had once known.

Just when I felt most defeated, in 2014, I was invited to be an instructor at Parsons School of Design, where I would have the pleasure of guiding graduate students enrolled in the strategic design and management programme. It was an opportunity to develop and share new methods for creativity and innovation— and to find the tools that would bring back my own creative practice. This would turn out to be a journey so rich it would lead to one of my proudest acts of making to date: this book, which I now see I have been carrying with me since those early days in the sandbox.

This book didn't begin as a book. I didn't strategise or plan it; that came later. Initially, this book came out of making. I began designing a deck of cards with exercises to help others avoid the suffering that comes with creative struggle. These practices were a way to guide lost creatives and beginners alike to (re)discover their creativity.

By the time I started designing and making scrappy prototypes of my creative card deck, I had been an instructor at Parsons for several years, teaching graduate students and giving career guidance. I listened as brilliant professionals and innovators at every level spoke about their longing to create and make an impact and about the frustrations of the creative struggle.

They felt hopeless, demotivated, and confused about where to go next and how to use their creativity to do it. Disconnected from their personal creative motivations, they had fallen into the same trap that I had found myself in years before.

I notice one common theme among the hundreds of people I have taught and collaborated with. Simply put, they have stopped making. And *not* making is affecting their capacity to innovate, collaborate, and find joy in every area of their lives. The less they practice, the more they procrastinate, and the more difficult it becomes to begin... And the deeper the creative longing grows.

When I finally returned to my creative practice at long last, I was stronger, wiser, and more intentional in my making—and determined to never lose my creativity again. This book is an attempt to share the strength I have felt in my return to creativity, and the practices that got me there, with you.

I built this book using every creative lesson I have learned up to now. My creative learning has spanned many terrains, from professional dance, music, and theatre training and performing to designing and launching a greeting card line, to my later career in entrepreneurship, design, and education. I offer up the highs and lows of my personal creative struggle to let you know you are not alone. The practices in this book are a gift to support you in your making practice so that you may face the creative struggle with confidence and live with the creative freedom you long for.

- Holly

Part 1:

Defining your creative context

Because your creativity is unique

Deciding to explore your creativity is a courageous move. It is a step into a world of uncertainty, where *you* define what's possible. Navigating the creative struggle is both exhilarating and terrifying. That's why it's important to start your journey knowing who you are, how you fit into the creative landscape, and how you can shape your environment to support your making. This will give you the solid base you need to build creative practices that work for you.

When it comes to your creativity, context matters.

In Part 1 of this book, you will explore your creative conditions and gain a better understanding of where your creativity is most needed and what's holding you back from living your best creative life. You'll identify what motivates you to create and define what creativity means to you. Finally, you'll discover your imaginator type, and learn how your unique imaginative strengths and vulnerabilities can help you to collaborate with your co-creators.

Once you've understood more about who you are and how your imaginative contributions fit into your surroundings, you'll be ready to face the creative struggle head-on and design a creative practice that fits your life (which we'll cover in Part 2). For now, let's start exploring your creative context!

Chapter 1
Creativity

What is it anyway?

>
> Creativity is a combinatorial force: it's our ability to tap into our 'inner' pool of resources—knowledge, insight, information, inspiration and all the fragments populating our minds—that we've accumulated over the years just by being present and alive and awake to the world, and to combine them in extraordinary new ways.

Maria Popova
Essayist, author, poet, and founder of *The Marginalian*

The twenty-first century has put creativity front and centre. The concept has been sensationalised, scrutinised, debated, and investigated, and in many professional environments, creativity has become *the* skill to cultivate. So what exactly is creativity anyway?

Creativity is primarily associated with the **arts or being an artist**. This definition also attaches importance to arts education and culture. At its essence, creativity in this context is understood as a deeply meaningful practice designed to be celebrated, revered, and shared. However, the artistic conception of creativity often emphasises individual talents or gifts, which in turn validates some as "creative" while rejecting others as "not creative".

The **business environment**, on the other hand, gives us the message that creativity is all about technology and innovation. In corporate settings, long debates take place on questions like, "Are you born with creativity?" "Is everyone creative?" "Can creativity be developed?" Creative methodologies such as design thinking and futures thinking have gained worldwide popularity in this sector as powerful problem-solving approaches in fields as diverse as marketing, product management, and tech development. Design thinking promises a new mindset that engages and develops your creative capacities while also helping to solve human-centred problems.

But for many, creativity for the purpose of innovation is a source of frustration as much as inspiration, due to pressure from employers and the market alike. Elevated standards and unrealistic expectations shape a creative-competitive mindset.

The Oxford English Dictionary defines creativity more broadly as "the use of imagination or original ideas to create something". But this assumes easy access to the imagination as well as the ability to take creative action. So what if you don't have this imaginative access? Or what if you struggle to act? Does this mean you are not creative—or that you can never become creative?

When I ask my students to **explain or define creativity**, the most popular answer, in all contexts, is "creativity means thinking 'outside the box'". I am never surprised by this answer: it is my first clue that students have a lot to understand about themselves and what it means to practice creativity. But thinking about what creativity is—and the boxes we put it into— is a wonderful place to begin as an educator.

There's one more common understanding of creativity: as something linked to **health, wellness, and personal well-being**. In this domain, creativity is defined as a channel to explore emotions. Here, creativity is not connected with talent or innovation. Instead, it is thought of as a tool for psychological and emotional development, something that helps us to become whole and healthy individuals.

There's one common thread across all definitions of creativity, in each and every context we've looked at: **people**. Although the meaning of creativity shifts among these groups or sectors, the main focus is always on the individual creative person.

So wouldn't that mean that the true definition of creativity is *you*? The path to creativity starts with exploring your impulses, influences, and relationship with yourself. There is no one else out there who can make and imagine as you do. So better to embrace your distinct differences and start taking ownership of how you define your creativity.

Creativity is you.

If you have yet to reflect on what makes you and your creativity unique, now is the time. Use the following pages to explore what creativity means to you. Don't hesitate to start making now. That means getting these pages dirty and leaving your mark inside this book.

What is your definition of *creativity*?
Write it here.

As you work your way through this book, come back to this page from time to time and read your defintition of creativity. How does it evolve with you?

"We are all of us, unique—each a unique pattern of creativity and if we do not fulfill it, it is lost for all time."

Martha Graham

Modern dancer and choreographer

Your creative family tree

Investigate your creative roots

use this space
to create

Start by sketching out your creative family tree. Create a visual representation of the people that have influenced you over the years. Once you begin to understand how you have been influenced by others, you can then add your own branch to the tree. Creating your own branch places you within the creative family and represents the continued growth of all the creative energy that has shaped you into the creative being you are today.

How does it feel to be connected to the people who have influenced you, and see yourself as part of a long list of creative contributors?

Your inner superhero (ine)

Connect to your creative super-strengths and vulnerabilities

Draw attention to the skills, talents, and personality traits that make you extraordinary and face the "kryptonite" that blocks your creativity.

Exercise these creative muscles:

Creative confidence
When you practice being comfortable with your inner superhero(ine) you will start noticing how the world needs you.

Imagination and making
The practice of combining imagination play with the building of tangible visuals develops your ability to move ideas into reality.

How to...

1. **Prepare your creation space.** Find a space where you can reflect and make. Be sure to bring your creative notebook and any making materials that inspire you—like markers, magazines, scissors, glue stick, coloured and textured papers, etc.
2. **Begin with reflection.** In your creative notebook, make two columns. Label one column "My super-strengths" and the other "My kryptonite". Now think about the characteristics and skills you possess that make you "super". Don't be shy. Write these in the super-strengths column. Next, think about the characteristics that cause you to feel vulnerable and place these in the "kryptonite" column.
3. **Imagine the Super-You.** Using your two lists, begin to imagine a new superhero(ine) that represents you. What superpowers do you possess? Who—or what—is your nemesis? How are you helping the world? When do you activate your superpowers? What is your background story?
4. **Stretch your imagination.** Play around and enjoy altering reality. Can you fly? Are you a super math genius who unlocks deep secrets to solve the world's most wicked problems?
5. **Name yourself.** What is your superhero(ine) name?
6. **Sketch your super emblem.** Draft a simple sketch of your superhero(ine) emblem. Remember, Batman has the bat signal and Superman wears an "S". What is the symbol that will represent you?
7. **Bring your superhero(ine) to life with a visual.** Using your making materials, or a digital program, create a visual of your superhero(ine). Design a look. Include super gadgets and don't forget your emblem. Add a super tag line or quote—like Spiderman's motto, "With great power comes great responsibility."
8. **Share your super story.** Share your superhero(ine) with others. Practice telling your story.

Chapter 2
Why creativity? Why not?

Your motivations for creativity

"

Asking 'Why?' can lead to understanding. Asking 'Why not?' can lead to breakthroughs.

Daniel H. Pink
Author and expert on business and human behaviour

One reason you may have lost your creative impulse or started procrastinating is that you don't know why you are trying to be creative in the first place. When you don't know *why* you are doing something, it often makes learning how to do it that much more overwhelming and mysterious. When you're disconnected from your personal motivations, you're often left paralysed, disinterested, doubtful, or even afraid, which makes it hard to know how to act or react in creative situations. It's much easier to activate your creativity when you can see the purpose or meaning in it.

So why creativity at all? What creative urges or pressures are calling you?

To begin understanding what drives you, you'll have to dig deeper. Ask yourself:

Why do I want creativity in my life? *What meaning does creativity hold for me?*
Why do I want to be more creative? *Where is my creativity needed?*
Why a creative practice? *What is missing from my creativity?*
Why did I pick up this book? *Where do I need help?*

Everyone has a distinct set of circumstances where creativity is required of them, and a unique set of reasons for wanting to develop their creative capacities. Any reasons you may have for engaging in a creative practice are valid and worthwhile: the answers to *why?* are infinite. Defining what creativity is for you is a decision you make alone—but actually *being creative* is closely bound up with your circumstances and the people who surround you. When reflecting on where your creativity is needed or what might be missing, you may start to see **how others impact or influence your authentic impulses** to create. Understanding who—or what—influences you can help you identify and overcome creative blocks or barriers.

How do the people close to you define creativity? What do they ask of you and your creative capacities? How does interacting with others conflict or mesh with your personal motivations to create?

Your true motivations
When you're trying to find answers to the big *why*, it's easy to get mixed up between *being* creative and producing *because of* your creativity. This confusion can lead to serious creative blocks. When personal and professional creative motives become intertwined, many people abandon their personal creative practices when being creative no longer feels satisfying or enjoyable at work. But **giving up your personal creative practice** launches a dangerous cycle. The less you create for yourself, the less creative you will feel, and the less creatively motivated you'll become both at work and in life. Feeling you're not being recognised for your creative efforts or having less creative freedom when collaborating with others can also squash your personal motivation to create and to further develop your imaginative capacities.

I've witnessed first-hand the collapse of many aspiring artists and entrepreneurs who lost sight of their true motivation to create and felt the disappointment of having their contributions repeatedly dismissed in the business world. The struggle is especially real for those working in creative industries like design or marketing, who must find ways to balance their unique talents with what is actually being utilised within a fixed business context that constantly tests and evaluates their creativity. Through my own personal experience transitioning from artist to entrepreneur, I learned just **how clouded our motives can become**. The suffering I felt in unknowingly abandoning my personal creative practice and my true reasons for making nearly broke me.

You can find your way back to your creative practice.

But how?

Get to the core of what makes your creativity tick.

In my work as a creative consultant, I have noticed that people are often unclear on their own motivations for creating and that they tend to focus all their energy on what they perceive as barriers to their creativity. When people don't first establish their reasons for creating, they quickly begin to lose their creative drive and end up lost, dissatisfied, overwhelmed, or creatively blocked. This is understandable: when you're disconnected from your *why* and your purpose is unclear, you'll see unnecessary obstacles to your creative capacities emerge.

One prime example of this is the relationship between money and creativity. Being creative costs nothing, but earning a living from your creativity can cost you everything if you place all your focus on the bottom line and desert your authentic creative urges. I've found that while many people cite a lack of finances as their reason for not pursuing a creative endeavour, they have trouble describing how they would use the money they think they need or what they'd do if they had it. Though convinced they require a certain type of compensation or funding, they begin to lose sight of *why* they want or need it in the first place. This common story shows how **concentrating on barriers instead of understanding your true motivation** can actually close the creative channels that will lead the way to untapped resources.

Creative blocks can become cement walls if we let them. That means it's crucial to release these blocks before they become all-consuming. Start by drilling down to the core of your creative desires.

What truly motivates you to create?

Keep it simple and try using one word to discover the core of your motivation. Be honest with yourself; no one reason is better than another. Here are some words to consider: fame, fortune, status, competency, pleasure, recognition, acceptance, spirituality, humanity, change, invention... and so on.

> "For true success ask yourself these four questions: Why? Why not? Why not me? Why not now?"
>
> **James Allen**
> Writer and moral philosopher

When you really understand your motivation, you can establish a clear vision that determines how you'll use your creativity and also how you'll set personal boundaries with others to support your creative needs.

Why not?
Once you've reflected on the question *why?*, next try shifting to *why not?*—You might discover that it is the list of *nots* that's holding you back from your full creative potential.

Asking *why not?* gives you a chance to examine all the *nots* and *nos* and *shoulds* and *should nots*—and then throw them out the window. *Why not?* turns a *no* into a *yes* and gives you permission to let go of the reasons you cannot do something. This frees you up to **believe in boundless possibilities**. This world of *yes!* invites you to embrace the process rather than centring on the outcomes.

Framing your practice with *why not?* offers a mindset of pure creative freedom. It emphasises exploration, reflection, and discovery, resulting in deeper self-expression and emotional connection. By resisting the importance of outputs, you'll also open up more space for personal satisfaction during the creative process. The joy and delight you experience while focusing on the process is **a welcome invitation for inspiration** to make a visit.

The main goal of working through *why?* and *why not?* is seeing that your reasons and motivations are valid. It's so easy to compare ourselves with others or listen to the voices of society, and even people close to us, telling us what we should or shouldn't aim for. In essence, understanding your personal motivation for creating lays a strong foundation by giving you clear expectations for yourself and establishing a secure space where you can safely grow your creativity. Knowing why you want or need to create will help you measure your growth as you build creative momentum, and let you keep tabs on your levels of satisfaction—and *dissatisfaction*—throughout the process.

Take a moment to reflect on your motivations. What are your answers to *why?* and *why not?* Write it down here.

It's okay to change

Your motivations are bound to change along the creative journey, and that's okay—even desirable. Therefore, it's important to reassess your creative intentions from time to time. Adjusting to a new *why* at any given moment is what makes you alive, human, and resilient. Being truly creative means being agile and open to change, which grows your capacity to accept your creative circumstances and *start from where you are.*

Chapter 3
Start from where you are

Your creative permission slip

"

You have to start from where you are today and from what can be done.

Simone de Beauvoir
Writer, existentialist philosopher, feminist activist, and social theorist

There is nothing more limiting to your creativity than not accepting yourself for who you are today. It's deeply harmful to your creative process to believe you need more of something before you can begin, and put off making until you have more resources, more talent, more time, more knowledge... the list can go on and on. Often, this list of excuses holds you back from opportunities to take action and live your creative life—*right now.*

Holding onto these excuses eventually results in creative paralysis. We get blocked by our own expectations—the aspirational future versions of ourselves or the stale narratives of our past that scream at us before we can even begin. "Stop!" they say. "This territory is dangerous!" These voices from the past may be connected to memories of failure or pain from previous creative attempts. But remember, you are a different person today. This present-day version of yourself—the **Today You**—can move on and grow out of yesterday.

Another harsh voice that pops up is that of the not-yet-realised **Future You**, who thrives when whispering endless *shoulds* in your ear. "You should be more accomplished. You should be more talented. You should be more creative", she threatens. Best to resist her *shoulds*.

Punishing yourself for not being where you think you should be—or would like to be— doesn't support your creativity.

If you start from where you are, and commit to using what you have at your disposal right now, you may eventually reach that future creative self you hope for. Even better: by meeting yourself where you are right now, you can **go beyond your current expectations of the future**, and, instead, allow yourself to evolve in the process and reach your full creative potential—which may look different than you think. Remember, each action you take in your journey will expand your creativity and develop your skills in a way that benefits and supports you unconditionally.

Starting from where you are is something you will practice every day of your creative life. But if you don't begin at all, your creativity will ebb away from the constant wanting.

When I was a young performing artist, my creative process suffered from the strict standards of perfectionism. I constantly looked to creative ideals and compared myself with others who were more experienced or more mature than me. Like most young artists, I had a vision for how I should—or could—be, and I wanted to fast-forward the process to be what I imagined for myself. My expectations not only limited my creative process but also robbed me of the joy of discovery that happens during the process, in the here and now.

In the professional theatre world, all actors learn about typecasting. This is when casting directors look for a "type", judging actors based on outward appearances or characteristics and slotting them into roles such as the ingénue, the comic, the mother, or the villain. Most young actors don't want to accept their "type"—either because the ego sees it as a threat against their talent, or because the actor is simply in the real-life process of discovering their own identity. Later down the line, the actor realises that by not accepting who they were in the moment, they missed out on opportunities to develop their craft, evolve their creativity, and eventually grow out of a type.

Typecasting is something all of us run into at some point in our lives, especially in our careers. Suggesting that you see your "type" as a reflection of who you are at a particular moment isn't to say that you need to stick to that role. But accepting where you are in your process and playing to your current strengths will benefit you in the long term. You will gain confidence and make more space for growing into the roles you aspire to play.

As I matured in my creative journey, so did my creative practice. I went from performing arts to visual arts, discovering new ways to create and collaborate along the way. During that process, I grew out of believing in "perfect". I learned that creation is best served by our imperfections, and what we can contribute comes from starting with who we are today.

The challenge to **start from where you are** is one you will continue to face every day if you choose to keep developing your creative capacities as you grow older. I will celebrate my forty-ninth birthday while writing this book, and in recent years I have faced a new chorus of internal voices singing, "You're too old."

Fortunately, I continue to find myself touched by the words of others who are grappling with the same voices alongside their own creative practices. They remind me it is never too late. In 2020, choreographer Darrell Grand Moultrie was rehearsing with professional dancer Linda-Denise Fisher-Harrell (who was 50 at the time) when she stopped during the process to realise that, instead of pushing through with how she thought she should dance, "...maybe I have to do something else... on *this* instrument", to which Darrell nodded his head in agreement and replied: "Honouring the instrument right in front of us."

> "Honouring the instrument right in front of us."
>
> **Darrell Grand Moultrie**
> Choreographer

This resonated with me on so many levels. Not only does the physical body change with age, but our ideas about ourselves and the world also evolve. Who you are right now is a unique gift, and your creativity does not judge you for your age or your stage in life.

Think of *starting from where you are* as a warm embrace. Acknowledging and accepting yourself in the present will open the door for you to **do great things with what you've got in this moment.** It helps you to seize every opportunity to be creative, even with the limitations in front of you. And the truth is, creative constraints are not limitations—they are gifts. What you see as obstacles are the exact resources you need today to fuel your creative process.

TRY THIS

Personal timeline

Honour the journey you are on

use this space
to create

Draw out a timeline showing your personal journey, starting with the day you were born and leading right up to this very moment. Include important milestones, achievements, pitfalls, and heartbreaks. Create a visual that tells the story of your life. Once you're finished, share your personal timeline with someone else. How does it feel to tell your story?

Reflect on how *who you are* and *where you have been* defines your **Today You.**

Chapter 4
Your creative context

Thinking about the box before thinking outside of it

"

Always design a thing by considering its next larger context—a chair in a room, a room in a house, a house in an environment, an environment in a city plan.

Eliel Saarinen
Architect

In my classrooms, the most common explanation students have for *creativity* is "thinking outside of the box". To which I always reply, "Well, what, then, is 'the box'?"

What I am reminding them is that you cannot begin to think with originality if you don't understand where you are creating from. People struggle most with the creative process when they choose to skip over one very important step—exploring their context. Without a firm grasp on your creative circumstances, there's a greater chance you'll find yourself running into cement walls during the creative process, which can leave you feeling disappointed and putting false blame on yourself when creativity fails.

Context is the box
Think of context as **everything happening in the world around you that affects your creative practices and your creative decision-making.** The most important factors to consider include

the people engaged with you in the process; your current conditions; your access to resources; and, finally, the systems and regulations that structure your creative efforts. Each of these factors influences your potential to make.

Scope of the context
Your creative approach will most likely vary based on your work context, your personal life, and the nature of your specific projects or personal creative endeavours. While who you are as a creative remains constant, **the variables affecting your creativity shift depending on the environment**. Think of the scope as the broader sense of the context. Before you begin moving inwards to explore the important factors that make the box, practice identifying the space the box sits within: its scope. Determine whether the context you're creating in falls under the scope of work, home, or the constraints of a very specific project. Defining the scope will help you stay focused on all that is happening within the context that directly influences your creative decision-making.

Build a box and make it visual
Creating a clear visual representation of your context will help you to explore your "box". Practice by using the activity spread on page 40 or a large piece of paper or whiteboard. You decide. The important part is that you start to build a visual model you can review and modify later on. Let's get started.

First, decide on a creative situation to map out. Draw yourself at the centre. Remind yourself of what makes you unique using what you've learned in Chapters 1, 2, and 3. Next, draw a square around yourself and label each of the four sides: people, conditions, resources, and systems. You see? You are inside a "box" of creative constraints that you will ultimately decide to work with, disrupt, or "think outside of". Finally, around the box you've sketched, draw a very large circle. Everything inside this circle will be your "scope". Be as clear as you can in mapping out this framework. Recognise that this map represents just one of the many scopes and boxes you will find yourself exploring through different projects and circumstances.

Now you are ready to investigate your creative context. Work through each one of the sides of your box adding details on the people, conditions, resources, and systems relevant to your creativity until your circle is filled. Use the following descriptions of these four key factors to guide you through.

1. People

Whether at work or at home, the people in our lives have an impact on how and when we create—and not everyone around you will be supportive of your creativity. It's a good idea to consider all the different groups of people who influence the resources and space you have for making. First, think of the people who inspire you, energise you, and offer their full support. What interactions do you have with these people? How do they reinforce your motivations for creating? Who helps you feel empowered? Next, think about those who discourage you and impose limitations, or those whose beliefs conflict with your motives to make. Is someone at work crushing your creativity? Why? Once you've made these two lists, include yourself on each of them, as appropriate. Do you have an inner naysayer or critic who spins narratives that support your procrastination, rather than your making and creating? When does your inner optimist do the talking?

2. Conditions

It's undeniable that the reality of our wider conditions at any given moment affects our ability to make. Factors like culture, position, credibility, power, perception, and timing all influence the dynamics of any potential creative project or collaboration. Also include the emotions you are carrying with you during the creative process, since **your creative context is always connected to your emotional state**. Conditions are not always permanent, although sometimes we may feel they are. Describe your conditions in detail.

3. Resources

Creative ideas require resources. Besides time—the creative person's most valuable resource—other key resources to support your making practice include creative tools or supplies, technology, and access to knowledge or people. List the resources you have at your disposal and the resources that you feel are missing.

4. Systems

Systems are built to help us, but they can create barriers when we're trying to innovate, disrupt, or design something new. Understanding the systems, rules, and regulations you're working within gives you a creative advantage. You need to **know the rules before you can break them**—and appreciate how a system works before you can change it. Even in cases when change isn't possible, understanding the system and learning how you can work within it empowers your creativity. Consider every level of the system and note who or what is responsible for building or changing it.

Making sense of context

Once you've explored the full context, it's time to step back and synthesise the information you've gathered so you can face the realities you are up against and spot any unseen opportunities. Identify which elements will be difficult to alter and which factors work together or against one another to shape your creative reality. Which are the true barriers in your creative context and which are only *perceived* creative blocks?

Context as creative constraints—building the box

Once you grasp the realities of your context, you can begin turning perceived limitations in your making process into creative constraints that structure, guide, and assist your creativity. These restrictions become the "box" we all speak of—and getting familiar with the box helps us identify opportunities to think outside of it. Creative constraints prepare the creation space and the mind, laying the groundwork for creative freedom.

Now that you have a box, you can start thinking outside of it!

Ideas also have contexts

We come up with ideas hoping that they'll find life in the real world. This world is vast and constantly changing and there are many overlapping **cultural, economic, and environmental factors that influence our creative outputs.** Therefore, context matters— and it's important to keep a pulse on how your creations fit into the world around you. When generating ideas, solving problems, or creating something new, start off by **exploring the wider contextual space in which your ideas are born.** Use the same process which you followed to map out your creative context, but this time, instead of placing yourself in the centre of your visual, put the idea in the middle, as the central focus. Then, imagine how your ideas will live in the world—and how they'll affect people, conditions, resources, and systems—once they are made.

Think about the box

Context as a source of creative constraints

use this space
to create

Practice investigating your creative context by making a visual map of your circumstances and environment. Use the guidelines in Chapter 4 to build your diagram of creative constraints—the "box"— that you will work with and learn to "think outside of". You can then review and refer to your "box" when making creative decisions.

Chapter 5
Who is behind the life of an idea?

Your imaginator type

"

Nothing is more powerful than an idea whose time has come.

Victor Hugo
Poet, novelist, and dramatist

Ideas are first conceived in the imagination space, where you begin to gather information and make sense of the inputs that surround you. Your imagination is your central hub for innovation, self-expression, and invention. When activated, your imagination is your most considerable creative gift. It is the source of your creativity. It is your superpower. All that you create relies on your imagination, and without it you simply cannot *be* creative.

But how do ideas come to life? What happens to them after they're first conceived?

If you've ever had a "great" idea that you wanted to turn into a reality, then you know what it means to face the creative struggle. The life of an idea, though, doesn't always depend on whether the idea itself is "good" or "bad". But it *does* depend on the people who bring it to life.

So, then, who is behind the life of an idea?

You are behind the life of an idea—you and all the others you collaborate with. Ideas, even when they emerge from the imagination of one single person, call upon the skills, motivations, and inspiration of many. In the realm of creative collaboration, I consider there to be three types of **imaginators**: *Idea Generators*, *Idea Makers*, and *Idea Implementers*. *Idea Generators* imagine new ideas by making connections between their observations and their own thoughts or reference points. Meanwhile, *Idea Makers* bring ideas to reality in palpable ways, by imagining how an idea could exist in the tangible world. Finally, *Idea Implementers* imagine how tangible ideas are connected to people and systems. It takes all three types, and access to their different forms of imagination, to breathe life into ideas. **What type of imaginator are you?**

What
type of
imaginator
are you?

Idea Generators

Idea Generators possess creative power because they have immediate access to their imaginations, which they use as a matter of habit. They are curious and inquisitive people who thrive on exploring their thoughts and enjoy spending time reflecting and ruminating on ideas. *Idea Generators* are observant and aware. They are quick to recognise problems and capable of coming up with rapid solutions in their mind's eye. They are never afraid to **travel deep within their imagination to envision things that may seem impossible to others.** The *Idea Generator* doesn't shy away from trying out new approaches or looking at things from a different perspective.

Idea Generators are naturals at *creating* ideas, but they often struggle with bringing their ideas to reality. However, it should be noted that not all *Idea Generators* struggle to plan out or act on their ideas.

Idea Makers

Idea Makers, on the other hand, are excellent at bringing ideas to fruition. Like *Idea Generators*, *Idea Makers* possess a large imaginative capacity. However, their strength is **using their imagination within the transition space between an idea as a *thought* and an idea as a *reality***. *Idea Makers* have a knack for connecting idea thoughts to tangible objects in the real world so that ideas can breathe life. In other words, they **love to make!** *Idea Makers* use their hands, along with all of the resources, materials, and space around them, to build prototypes of what has been imagined. They often prefer working within creative constraints because these restrictions inspire more creative choices. *Idea Makers* have a close relationship with the [im]possibilities of their surroundings, and they have a talent for creating new solutions from existing objects and resources.

The challenges that *Idea Makers* face are usually tied to the *implementation* of their imaginative creations. A lack of resources to scale their ideas, or insufficient manpower to put prototypes into action, can sometimes limit the power of a made idea.

Idea Implementers

This is where **Idea Implementers** make their creative debut. *Idea Implementers* are good at connecting relationships, systems, and people with ideas. They are big-picture thinkers, who look for connections between ideas and understand how creativity lives in the real world. *Idea Implementers* use their imagination to visualise new contexts and scenarios where ideas can interact with people and the wider environment.

Believe it or not, *Idea Implementers* can find it difficult to come up with ideas, which is where *Idea Generators* thrive. *Idea Implementers* flourish when they can take existing creative ideas through to implementation, and create new contexts for those ideas to exist.

As you can see, *Idea Generators*, *Idea Makers*, and *Idea Implementers* all rely on each others' collaboration to see ideas through from thought to actuality. Each type of imaginator works within their own imaginative capacities and *stretches* these capacities to contribute to the life of ideas.

Once you know what type of imaginator you most resemble, then think about how you collaborate with other types. How can you work with other imaginators' strengths and vulnerabilities? Don't be afraid to ask other creative types for their help. It's okay to not know everything; this is why we collaborate! Through creative collaborations, we can learn from one another and share our creative superpowers so more ideas can come to life.

Use the prompts on the following page to understand what imaginator type(s) you fit most. You may find a piece of yourself in every type.

Imaginator types

Cross-pollinate expertise

use this space
to create

What type(s) of imaginator are you? What are your creative strengths and challenges? How do you own them in your creative process? Start by listing five super-strengths, or things you are good at, that support your imaginator type, and write down five reasons you feel vulnerable in co-creation spaces. Then, introduce yourself to someone you believe is a different type from you. Discover ways you can collaborate and support one another in the creation process.

Build a diverse team of imaginators. Bring an idea to reality.

They just don't understand what *we* do.

Creatives vs. non-creatives

I have been working with "non-creatives" long enough to understand why people choose to label themselves this way, especially in the workplace. In an environment where artistic people and businesspeople are clearly separated by responsibilities, titles, and office space, it is naturally more difficult for the "non-creative" to get any practice generating and communicating ideas. On the other side of things, the "creative" employee often ends up frustrated because their ideas never see the light of day in terms of implementation.

One of the stories I hear most often is that of miscommunication or missed connections between those we generally call "creative" and those who are designated as "non-creative". Both claim: "*They* just don't understand what *we* do." I have observed many projects where each side blames the other and frustration grows. But the gap between these two worlds has less to do with the creative capacities of "creatives" vs. "non-creatives" than with **how different imaginator types collaborate with one another.**

Understanding your collaborators' distinct creative inclinations and imaginative strengths, as well as your own, supports the process of imagination and honours all people as creative. Imagine what we could accomplish if we paid attention to where others feel most comfortable during the creative process and respected where our collaborators need additional practice.

Build better co-creation relationships

Cross-team collaboration and cross-pollination of our expertise demands a lot from us. It requires learning new languages and new skills. It asks us to be empathetic and curious. It calls on us to share knowledge, and teach and lead others who need more practice. It's a tall order, especially with deadlines and clients and corporate goals mixed into the creative process. But it can be done. Accepting the beginner in yourself and embracing the beginner sitting across from you is an excellent way to begin a co-creation relationship.

The more we know about where we feel most comfortable in imaginative processes, and where we need additional practice, the better we can manage our individual creative capacities and feel confident when collaborating with other imaginator types.

Note: your collaborators' imaginator types may not be what you think. While most "non-creatives" are considered great *Idea Implementers*, many others are just dying to show off their inner *Idea Generator* or *Idea Maker*. Never underestimate the creative potential of others. Instead, take the time to be curious about your co-creators. Practice feeling comfortable saying these phrases: "I don't know." "Could you teach me?" "Let me help you."

Everyone loves to show off their inner superhero(ine), but we can make our kryptonite work for us, too. The next time you find yourself saying "I don't know", try seeing your own shortcomings as an opportunity to connect with others while exploring new territory.

Begin with yourself
Now that you understand more about where you fit into the creation of ideas, work on improving the areas you feel less comfortable with.

- **Idea Generators** can practice taking creative action by making things.
- **Idea Makers** can practice investigating new contexts where ideas can fit into the world.
- **Idea Implementers** can practice accessing the imagination space and generating ideas.

You can use the exercises in the last section of this book to strengthen underutilised creative muscles.

Practice using the creative challenge on the following page to improve co-creation flow between you and your fellow imaginators.

Co-creation flow

Practice creating with others

Share the creative process with others and exercise your capacity to listen to your co-creators and let go of sole ownership of ideas. Focus not on what you create but rather focus on how you create *together*.

Exercise these creative muscles:

Listening
Practice opening your ears and your mind to how your co-creators are approaching the process and the suggestions they are inviting you to take.

Embracing the uncomfortable
Exercise managing your feelings when faced with uncomfortable suggestions. Practice accepting the perspectives of others to grow your capacity to embrace and respect the ideas of co-creators.

How to...

1. **Choose a partner.** Find someone (or a small group of co-creators) that you can create with. Challenge yourself to work with different imaginator types.
2. **Find a space.** Try looking for a neutral location or a space that both people agree fosters creative action. This creation space could be anywhere ranging from a studio or *makerspace* to a simple space such as your kitchen table or an online Zoom call. The most important thing to consider when choosing a space is that both co-creators feel comfortable (or equally uncomfortable) in the space.
3. **Set up your creative constraints.** No need to focus on what you will create. Best to start by agreeing on the starting point for entering this creative partnership. Together, develop a small list of creative constraints (boundaries, guidelines). For example, choose 3-5 materials you will use to co-create with. Or set other types of boundaries, such as time constraints or choosing a specific context or theme. Setting creative constraints is your first chance to practice working together.
4. **Begin creating together.** Use your creative constraints as a launching pad for creation. Remember to stay focused on the creation process and not the end result.
5. **Be open.** Practice listening to one another. Use the "Yes, and..." technique. When your partner shares an idea you reply, "Yes, and how about...?" Exercise your capacity to let go of what you think it should be and try using new ways to approach the process (thanks to your partner!). Ask one another questions. Use "What if?" and "How might we...?" to look at ideas from different angles.
6. **Trust.** Observe the creative process that takes place when someone else is engaged with you. Trust that process and practice trusting one another to lead it.
7. **Don't finish.** Practice not showing a final product. Try stopping before you have reached any final conclusion.
8. **Talk about it.** Take time to talk about your experience sharing the creative process. Take turns sharing and listening to one another. Include what it felt like not to finish a project together. Did not finishing give you the freedom to be more creative during the process? Did not finishing cause you to feel frustration (or any other feelings)?

Chapter 6
Creative struggle is real

And we love it!

"

Man's creative struggle, his search for wisdom and truth, is a love story.

Iris Murdoch
Novelist and philosopher

Creativity is a glorious beast that fills us with inspiration only to strip it away and then hand it back to us better than before. Attempting to make something from nothing is both exhilarating and excruciating. I know. I have been doing it for nearly five decades, and I *still* love it!

The seed of an idea or creative desire can take over your life. From inception to realisation, we willingly engage in the uncertainty of the creative process. There, we must overcome doubts and fears, and recover from the exhaustion of balancing our creative intentions with life's distractions. The longing to make an impact and put our creative capacities to good use is all-consuming, especially when working with co-creators and clients in creative work environments. And when a creative endeavour fails to meet its potential or when we fall short of reaching our dreams, we experience a form of grief.

The creative struggle is real. So very real that it hurts sometimes. And just when you think it's taken you down, it nudges you to rise up again. Which is why we choose to face this struggle again and again, with pleasure.

Pursuing the creative struggle with all its pains, as well as pleasures, is what it truly means to be creative.

But what if you could face the struggle like a superhero? What if you could train yourself to face creative encounters with a confident approach?

In the fast-paced environments of business, innovation, science, and technology, and the complex systems of educational institutions, we are asked to "create, create, create!" in a way that pushes us away from our unique creative voices and forces us to perform, ideate, produce, and problem-solve toward rushed creative outputs. Demanding clients and bosses can stifle or block our creativity.

The creative struggle we tackle in this book, though, isn't the one you have with your boss or your fellow team members or clients. It is the struggle you alone face within the creative process. It's how you view yourself, when you feel "creative" or "not creative", and how you understand your creative potential and whether or not you are living up to it. It is **the unique creative calling that you have within yourself to create change, make an impact, be curious, and explore the world.**

Every creative endeavor we embark on sets us up for opportunity and a world of possibilities. To embrace the creative struggle is to take creative action—and isn't that what we are all striving for? Rather than ignoring or suppressing it, facing up to your unique creative struggle is the best way to live as closely as possible to your authentic creative self and share your creativity with the world.

In Part 1, you defined your own reasons to "create, create, create". In Part 2, you'll learn to work *with* the struggle by developing a rhythmic creative practice that will help you turn your creative chaos into rocket fuel so you can reach your full creative potential.

Take a moment now to befriend your creative struggle by acknowledging it exists. Get it out on paper. Use the exercise on the next page.

Befriend the struggle

Embrace the tension and enjoy the process

use this space
to create

Embrace the tensions, emotions, and uncertainties that come with engaging in the creative process. Acknowledge that the creative struggle is a struggle—and use its energy to boost your creativity. Use the space below to describe the struggles you are having with your creativity.

When acknowledging the struggle, what is most difficult to accept and why?
What methods do you currently use to face the struggle?
What delights you about the creative struggle?

Designing your creative practice

To *be* creative, you have to *do* creative

The space between doing and not doing can be overwhelming—which often makes navigating the creative struggle feel impossible.

If you worked through the exercises in Part 1, you should now have a better understanding of what makes your creativity tick, what impact you want your creative contributions to make, and what your unique creative struggle looks like.

In Part 2 of this book, you'll learn to work *with* the struggle rather than against it by developing a steady creative practice that follows the right rhythm for you. You'll be able to use practical strategies to face your doubts, insecurities, or sense of creative chaos with a new confidence that will help you build creative momentum that lasts.

There's no "magic bean" for creativity. This second section of the book is designed for the curious, the committed, and perhaps even the *obsessed* maker who is willing to put in the hard work it takes to practice living a creative life and invite creativity into their daily existence, little by little.

By trying out the creative challenges and making the effort to exercise your creative muscles, you'll find a source of creative rocket fuel you can take back to work, where you will perform better, collaborate better, and feel better. Let's go!

Chapter 7
What is a creative practice?

Choosing a style that works for you

"

Your voice develops as a result of showing up and making stuff, not once or twice, but over and over and over again.

Lisa Congdon
Artist, author, and illustrator

Not creating doesn't mean you don't *know* how to be creative. It could be that you're simply not doing it often enough. Whether you're trying to build a new skill or hoping to develop an original idea, you can really only be creative when you are actually creating. Yet even though we know this to be true, we still let ourselves procrastinate on our creative intentions or fail to engage in the creative process on a regular basis. I know first-hand how intimidating the space between doing and not doing can be. So how can we navigate this emotional territory?

Although successful creativity is often misleadingly associated with chaotic behaviour or freely doing whatever you want, whenever you want, while waiting for inspiration to strike, believe it or not, **your creativity actually thrives when it is given structure**. Working within a framework that provides repetition and ground rules supports your process and opens up space for more creative possibilities.

By establishing a creative practice, you can build this structure and find new ways of organising yourself that grant you the time and space to develop your creative capacities, grow your potential, make an impact, and share your creative voice. A healthy practice requires you to exercise your creative muscles regularly. With your creative muscles "in shape", you'll then be able to take advantage of your imaginative capacities to execute original ideas and find new contexts where your creativity can be applied.

What is a creative practice?

A creative practice is the intentional repeated act of entering a creative process with the support of your creative mindset.

Let's break it down...

- **mindset = thinking** (beliefs, motivation, attitudes, intentions)
- **process = exploring** (imagining, acting, making, experimenting, discovering)
- **practice = repeating** (habits, iterations, attempts, rehearsal)

Think back to Part 1 of this book and review what you learned about yourself and your creative mindset. How do your motivations inform your methods for making? Take a moment to reflect on your creative process. How often are you exploring? Begin to think about the creative habits you currently keep and see where there's room for change. Remember to **start from where you are**.

Creative practices, and the motivations behind them, come in all shapes and sizes. Your practice is as unique as you are, and there is no right or wrong way of doing it. Moving forward, in this section of the book, you'll focus on shaping a creative practice that is right for you.

While the design of a creative practice is distinctive to each individual, all practices share a common basis: **the act of forming habits that you repeat often**. The benefit of building creative habits is that you'll shape your thinking into a mindset that is curious, critical, and imaginative. The most successful creative practitioners develop a daily routine where they set aside a time and place each day to create *repetitively*. Repetition means you will do it again and again... and again.

Practice demands that you repeat things that bore you or frustrate you. Practice means facing your vulnerabilities and, sometimes, realising that you'll never outgrow them. Practice requires you to push yourself when things stagnate or get too comfortable.

Not every creative act requires the same amount of energy and not every individual creates in the same way. We are all beginners when it comes to our creativity. This is not because we don't know how to create, but because every day that we engage in the creative process, we choose to approach uncertainty. **In this territory of unknowns, we are met with wicked surprises that both delight and challenge us**. This is a space full of endless possibilities that can only be accessed when we build a mindset of openness, agility, and willingness to face the unfamiliar. This, too, takes practice.

Finding a unique rhythm that works for you will not only help you to pick up speed and build creative momentum, but it will also make your practice a creative companion that you can rely on.

The fact that practice requires hard work doesn't mean that it shouldn't also be satisfying and enjoyable. Never forget that practice is just that—*practice*! It is not a performance. This is your space to make big mistakes, be messy, and not know what you are doing. Every day of practicing is a new day to explore, discover, and take pleasure in the life of your creativity.

The benefit of building creative habits is that you'll shape your thinking into a creative mindset that is curious, critical, and imaginative.

Different approaches and styles

You may be entirely new to exploring your creative capacities, or perhaps you're just starting to identify your own style or approach to your creative practice. Below, I introduce some of the more widely used approaches.

> "The truly prolific artists... have figured out a daily practice... they have all identified what they want to spend their time on, and they work at it every day, no matter what."
>
> **Austin Kleon**
> Author, artist, and creativity expert

Try one or all of them on for size—and, of course, feel free to go ahead and develop your own!

1. Repeated technique
2. Small steps
3. Everyday thinking
4. Create to create
5. Mixed methods

Repeated technique

This is the most common type of practice for someone trying to improve a specific technique or a creative skill set. The most common users of this approach are artists, but it's not limited to the realm of the "*artiste*". This style will support *anyone* trying to improve an artistic or creative skill, such as illustration, playing the piano, or dancing.

In this type of practice, you develop and strengthen your creative muscles by repeating tasks within a specific method or medium. That might be repeatedly playing an instrument or solving different creative puzzles. You do this on a daily basis until you achieve a certain level of growth or mastery—or, **until enough experimentation has occurred to result in a creative breakthrough or "aha!" moment.**

This kind of practice works for all levels of ability and experience. For instance, someone just beginning to play piano may practice their scales and finger positions every day before they can begin playing simple songs. An advanced concert pianist, on the other hand, who has mastered the basics of piano playing, would use this approach in a very different way. The experienced musician understands that they must practice with their instrument every day to maintain a relationship with the piano that will allow them to play more difficult pieces. Rehearsing a complex piece of music each day over time builds muscle memory that allows musicians to go beyond the basics and add their unique sense of musicality.

Thirty-day challenges, where you commit to training a certain technique every day for 30 consecutive days, are a great way to jumpstart this type of creative practice. Thirty consecutive days is enough to build momentum with a new skill and observe small improvements. You can use the activity spread *Your 30-day challenge* on pages 114–115 of this book to help.

More than the arts—build a creative toolbox
This approach is used for much more than building on talent or committing to desirable artistic hobbies. You can use this type of creative practice to establish a creative skill set or "toolbox" that is designed to expand your imaginative capacity and to improve your ability to develop ideas and solve complex problems. Start building your toolbox by repeating any one of the exercises in this book.

Small steps

This style of creative practice invites a slow and steady approach to achieving creative goals or changing your life. The practice of taking small steps is about including just a little bit more of that one thing you love into your life somewhere, somehow, every single day.

This approach to creativity is great for anyone who wants to make a life change or who has a specific creative goal in mind. The foundation of this approach is understanding that *change takes time.* **Investing consistent small bits of energy in your creative practice each day is like building a house brick by brick.** This approach honours the process and sets you up to face challenges without a huge amount of risk.

A practice like this is a good fit for people who are managing several projects or responsibilities at once. This type of creative practice asks for a small amount of time from you each day, which can relieve the pressure to tackle a big project under unrealistic circumstances.

For example, let's say you want to explore a new business idea, write a blog, or take on a large-scale creative project. With a "small steps" approach, you don't have to stop everything and obsess about the new creative endeavour. Instead, you can chip away at it day by day over a long period of time. Do you want to start a blog? Dedicate 15 minutes every day to reading other blogs, thinking of themes to write about, actually writing, or starting the process of establishing your blog space online. The point is, you don't have to drop your life and do it all at once. Take things one baby step at a time. Enjoy the process of letting your idea or intention evolve slowly but surely.

Everyday thinking

This type of creative practice is less about actions or building things and more about your thinking approach. The "everyday thinking" practice applies your creative mindset to all that you do throughout the day, ensuring that you are more aware of your surroundings and intentional about inviting in fresh perspectives. Activating a creative mindset in your daily life requires tapping into your curiosity and asking questions more often.

Exercises that stretch the imagination or train your emotional intelligence are perfect for this type of practice. Start with the creative challenges *Mashups* and *Headlines from the Future* on pages 80–83, as well as *Make your emotions* on pages 122–123.

For those working in—or leading—creative teams, this approach is an excellent fit. As you learned in Chapter 5 about collaborating with the different imaginator types, **everyone has their own way of thinking and creating**. The "everyday thinking" practice, when shared in groups or teams, is an effective way to cultivate a work culture that thinks and acts with an open mind.

Create to create

This is a creative practice driven by the process and nothing else. The main goal here is to drop your attachment to creative outcomes and instead make things solely for the sake of making or as a way of answering your questions and giving free reign to your curiosity.

This approach will also help you to find new frames and fresh perspectives by creating new iterations of existing ideas, and it's especially useful for designers and strategic teams focused on problem-solving. However, *everyone* can benefit from reinventing and repurposing otherwise old ideas. Practice using the creative exercise *Revisit, repurpose, reinvent* on pages 138–139.

This practice is a wonderful use of time and will also support anyone working on a health and wellness practice. Creating for no other purpose than to create is a useful tool for connecting with your emotions and getting in a creative flow, which can help to reduce stress.

Mixed methods

Beginner creative practitioners may find it best to choose one of the above practices and get started with it—for now. More experienced creative practitioners may want to take an approach that brings together aspects of all of these styles, to build a creative practice that ultimately fills your life and gives you a creative toolkit for every situation.

A "mixed methods" approach engages each of the different styles as and when they are most needed, allowing makers to flow between distinct methods with ease. For example, you may want to utilise the "repeated technique" to hone a specific skill that can help support your "everyday thinking" in teams, while also using a "create to create" methodology to relieve stress and stay motivated.

It's okay if you're not yet ready to take on a mixed-methods approach. It takes a generous amount of creative rehearsal time to start developing your creative capacities and learning how to adapt to life's circumstances and the creative constraints that come your way.

Practice does not make perfect, but it will help you grow, and, ultimately, the more you practice the more creative you will "be".

Keep calm and create

Remember: being creative doesn't mean that every time you sit down to take creative action you need to produce a result, finished product, or work of art. The creative process welcomes unfinished works in progress. Think of your "practice" as a warm-up or an exercise routine that strengthens your creative muscles each day to prepare you for the moment when you're ready to develop a more finalised concept or bring an idea to fruition.

If you are new to developing a creative practice, I strongly recommend that you assign a fixed time slot for your creative practice, whichever practice method you choose. Finding a regular time every day helps you to build a relationship with your creativity. That appointed time slot becomes your creative companion—a creative collaborator waiting each day to motivate you, saying: "No excuses. Let's create!"

While continuing to practice over weeks and months, you will discover that the concept of showing up for your creativity regularly eventually becomes an organic way of being. As your creative momentum begins to spill out into other areas of your life, both personally and professionally, you will no longer think about being creative; you will just *be*.

Chapter 8
Make space for creativity

Prepare for your practice

> **"**
>
> *In order to be creative you have to know how to prepare to be creative... a lot of habitually creative people have preparation rituals linked to the setting in which they chose to start their day. By putting themselves in that environment, they begin their creative day.*

Twyla Tharp
Dancer, choreographer, and author

Preparing yourself for your creative practice determines how satisfied you'll feel with your creative process—and ultimately defines how you view your creativity. Good preparation requires dedication to making yourself present for your creativity each day, designing spaces that inspire you, and finding the necessary tools and materials to support your creative intentions. Different people will relate differently to each of these elements, and will need to make individual decisions around how to design a process to help them prepare to create. This chapter will give you all the information you need to understand how best to prepare for your practice—use the space on pages 72–73 to design your unique space.

Commitment and intentions

Your *commitment* to practice is a pact that you make with yourself to show up for your creativity every day. Your *intentions* are the decisions you make within your practice, geared toward developing and enhancing your creative capacities. Each intention may have a special purpose—you may choose to focus on goals such as growing your curiosity or aiming to make something every day. If you need help setting intentions, you can go back and review Chapter 2 to understand the *why? and why not?* behind starting your creative practice.

Your personal commitment and creative intentions help you set milestones you can use to measure your creative progress and growth. They are also excellent reminders of your underlying motivations when distractions pop up or doubt creeps in. In difficult moments, your intention is there to say, "Don't stop! Don't give in! *This* is why you should show up and keep trying."

A little trick I use to support my creative intentions is to attach the objective to a physical object so that every time I see it, I'm reminded of my original reasons for starting. For example, when I wanted to commit to reading more books on a particular topic, I invested in a special yellow chair that would be dedicated to reading time alone. I gave the chair additional power by giving it a name: *The Golden Throne*. Using an object as a signal to act on my commitments holds me accountable. When I see the chair, I am not only reminded that my reading list is waiting, but I am also invited to sit down, take the time, and achieve what I set out to do. You could also do this with a tool or platform such as Instagram or Vimeo, and set an intention to share your progress as a part of your creative process. **Objects and tools can become creative companions.**

Time

Time is a creative person's most valuable resource. Scheduling time each day for your creative practice sets the pace for your creativity and helps build your creative momentum. Managing how you spend your time sets practical expectations for what you can accomplish or work on each day, which leads to more creative satisfaction.

The most successful creative people stick to a regular creative schedule by carving out a set block of hours focused purely on imagining and making. This method helps **stave off distractions so you can feed your focus and build creative flow**. Beginners may find a large chunk of time overwhelming, so I encourage you to start small. Start by setting a timer for 5–20 minutes each day to practice showing up for yourself and your creative practice. Then, train yourself to access your creative action points during that time frame (you'll learn more about using your creative action points in the next chapter). For now, you can use simple creative prompts as warm-ups or as a method to launch yourself into the process of creating. Once you get used to the time commitment and action steps, you can decide if you want to go deeper and spend more time exercising and training your creative muscles. Turn to the creative challenges at the end of the book to help build more strength.

Creative training takes time so don't be hard on yourself if, at first, finding your groove feels uncomfortable. What's most important is that you develop the consistency that your practice requires. Setting aside a specific time each day to activate your creative process shouldn't feel like a punishment. Instead, think of time constraints as a form of welcome guidance to keep you focused and lead you to your highest creative potential.

Space

The space you design for your practice is an essential ingredient to setting yourself up for creative success. Each person needs a unique space—a creative sanctuary—where creative rituals can take place and where you can take ownership of your creative process.

Your space will become your collaborative partner and co-creator. It should feel comfortable, like a trustworthy friend, and support your creative needs in the best possible way. Building a physical and mental space for your practice is a strong step toward becoming an active creative practitioner. Think of the physical space that you create as **the portal between your thought space and the creative imaginings you want to make a reality.** By dedicating a physical action space to exploration and discovery, you create an active channel for your imagination to play and for inspiration to arrive.

Think about how your body will react to the space and the effect this will have on your creative mindset and creative process. Is it filled with light? Does the space require silence, or do you need to be able to play music? These environmental details can become portals to inspiration, or they can hinder you by creating subconscious blocks.

The use of your space—or spaces—is at the heart of the interdisciplinary approach to making I propose to you throughout this book. Observe how it feels to move through different spaces in your practice. The actions you take within the space can also become the source of positive creative challenges. For example, instead of working from a desk, choose to work on the floor. What does it feel like to explore an object sitting on the ground instead of using a chair? If you focus on your body in your making practice, how does your approach to creative collaboration change? Reflect on how sharing your creative process with your new collaborator, *the space*, shifts and inspires a new approach to your creative actions and process.

Unique spaces for different activities

Across my creative lifetime, I have encountered spaces that support thinking and making and others that stifle the creative process. I now have a set of different spaces I use for different creative actions because I've come to understand that **not all creative acts demand the same from a space.** I love writing in what I call my *Golden Throne*. As mentioned previously, this is a bright yellow chair and ottoman specifically designated to my reading and writing activities. For me, this space works best when it is accompanied by peace, quiet, and as few interruptions as possible.

I also have a *Making Station*, which consists of a table and creative art supplies such as watercolours, markers, scissors, scraps of paper, and glue. In this space, I practice short creative sprints and focus on creative exploration. This is a no-pressure zone dedicated to embracing creative accidents. This area supports the *create to create* approach described in Chapter 7.

As a former dancer and actor, I have rehearsed in many dance studios and theatre spaces. To this day, I love how held I feel when I walk into an empty dance studio. The wide open floor and high ceilings beg for movement, and the walls, floor-to-ceiling windows and mirrors embrace me. The design of this space makes me want to dance, whether alone or with others, in a class or creative rehearsal process. The smell of sweaty inspiration, the marks on the floor from dance steps that came before me, and perhaps a piano or turntable in the corner all motivate me to move my body. The space itself inspires. The dance studio feels like a safe space for exploration. The elements of the dance rehearsal space—as opposed to the performance space—support my creative process and my craft.

Lastly, I have designed collaborative creative workstations to create with others. My desk with my computer and notebooks is a space dedicated to virtual collaborations. When co-creating with others in person, we look for large open tables where conversation and making can happen, and whiteboards or walls where "creative chaos" can unfold and later be organised. Depending on the necessary creative tools needed, other collaborative spaces can include labs or workshops, music studios, or rehearsal spaces.

Through working in creative industries my entire life, I've gotten used to building dynamic spaces with the appropriate tools and materials. But I have also experienced the limitations of locations where the needs of making and creating are not understood, fostered, or supported, whether these are temporary or permanent workspaces. This requires another type of preparation which falls to the responsibility of your creative mindset. **Even in the most unwelcoming circumstances, there is always room for creativity.** Do not let less-than-ideal situations cloud your reasons for diving in and making.

Now it's time to begin imagining and designing your unique creation space or spaces.

Explore your options

There are infinite ways to build creative spaces, and you will find yours by exploring different spaces and the objects that belong in them. It's not necessary to have a professional creative space dedicated solely to one creative practice, such as a studio of art, dance, music, or design, or *makerspace*, lab, or woodshop. Your creative space can be as simple as a notebook, a designated chair, or a shoebox.

Bring your tools

Much of the design of your creative space will depend on the tools that you will fill it with. **Your tools are an extension of your creative inquiry and self-expression.** Bring all the items necessary to support your making motivation. If you think you are missing certain tools that you don't have access to at the moment, make a wishlist but don't let that hold you back from preparing your creation space.

Remember, the creative process doesn't focus on outcomes and results. Use tools for exploration, and try new prompts and mediums. If you always work with digital tools, take a stab at adding analogue tools to your practice. Stay open to the unexpected that comes with creative intention and practice.

Make it your own

You may want to decorate your space and fill it with objects, inspirational quotes, and images that will motivate you. Arranging your creative tools in ways that fit your personality makes creating fun! Managing the details gives you ownership of the space. Do you require light and music, a beautiful view, or a cosy pillow? These details make a difference. They are your creative support team.

Your creative space should feel like home: a place where you belong. If you like messy, then be messy. If you prefer a super organised space, then be super organised. Be the ruler of your own creative castle.

Link time and space

Time is directly connected with how you choose to develop your space. Think about when you will use the space. For example, you may assign a table to be used for creative actions, but only on the weekends. Or you could create a space where you can be alone to create for 5 or 10 minutes every day. Pay attention to how you'll use your time when designing your space to help you stay motivated to return to it each day.

Start designing your creative spaces on the following page.

Your unique spaces

Designing your creative sanctuary

use this space
to create

Use the space below, and the guidelines in Chapter 8, to imagine and design your unique making space or spaces. Add visuals such as sketches, photos, or a collage to make it come to life. Think about how you will link the use of your time to the space.

The time for creativity is always.

Creative pop-ups

Creative pop-ups are a great way for beginners to carve out space for creativity. Use a temporary pop-up space that is available to you at any time during the day. **Knowing that you have this space sends signals to your brain that creativity is ready to happen.**

Imagine you have committed 5–20 minutes each day to your creative practice.

Use one of these creative pop-up spaces to make room for making:

- A cosy chair, a creative notebook, and your morning coffee.
- Space on your work desk before your colleagues arrive.
- A quiet meditation corner to practice accessing your imagination.
- A shoebox, a container, or a little bag that holds your favourite creation tools or games (storytelling dice, creativity card deck, etc.).
- Your mobile device and a social media app, where you create and share something.
- A daily walk to find inspiration and access your imagination.
- A computer or iPad or other designated tech tool or creation app.
- A small corner of the room or a special space dedicated to movement and short dance breaks.

The key to making a creative pop-up work for you is about letting go of the expectations that a creative space has to be big, fancy, or "ideal". Remember, the most important part of creating is showing up!

Overcome limitations

Sometimes our idea of a perfect creative space isn't always possible. Be open to trying out new ways to *pop-up* and show up. Work willingly within your creative constraints. You may have a roommate, a partner, a colleague, children, or a family that doesn't "fit" your perfect creative space. That's okay. Work with it. Don't let anything or anyone stop you from finding new ways to practice.

If space is tight, you can downsize your creative pop-up until more room becomes available or find space outside of your living area. Join a co-creation space, a class, or a club. Explore a coffee shop, a park bench, or your car! Wherever you make room for your creative pop-up, you are making room for your creative contributions to happen.

All things are possible when you make the space.

Are you all set up for creative success?

Before beginning the next chapter, take a moment to review how prepared you are by checking off the basics:

- ☐ I am committed to starting my creative practice.
- ☐ I have prepared a space for my creative practice to take place.
- ☐ I have a designated time slot for my creativity.
- ☐ I plan to engage in some form of creative practice every day.

Now watch your creative momentum build.

Chapter 9

Activate your creative capacities

Imagine. Make. Connect. Reflect.

> **"**
> *This world is but a canvas to our imagination.*

Henry David Thoreau
Poet, essayist, and philosopher

There are four key moments that activate your creativity within your creative process. I call these the *four creative action points: imagine, make, connect, and reflect.*

Each of these is essential to the life of your ideas and the evolution of your creativity. When approaching your creative process, you may discover that some action points come more naturally than others. This is normal, and just means that you have a little work to do to exercise any underdeveloped areas.

This chapter will guide you through these four critical elements and show you how they can help you develop a solid creative practice, deepen your creative mindset, and **connect to your unique imaginative strengths and vulnerabilities**. You may want to look back at your superhero(ine) from Chapter 1 and your imaginator type from Chapter 5 to refresh your memory.

Each creative action point will help you to activate a different aspect of your creativity.

1. **Imagine:** enter the imagination space more easily and expand your exploration of the impossible.
2. **Make:** move the imaginary into physical space by building tangible prototypes of your ideas.
3. **Connect:** share your imagined ideas, your scrappy prototypes, and your curiosities with others, and exercise your storytelling skills.
4. **Reflect:** follow an intentional rumination practice by documenting thoughts, feelings, insights, and questions about your creative process in real time.

Imagine

Your imagination is your creative superpower. With imagination, all is possible. The *imagine* creative action point refers to the primary moment when your creativity is unlocked.

In the imagination space, you are free to visualise what does not yet exist. This could mean imagining something that seems impossible to you in the present—maybe you'll find yourself envisioning a futuristic time machine or a living, breathing unicorn. Here, your activated imagination encourages you to dream and play. But as well as dreaming up the impossible, we use imagination to picture things in our mind's eye even when they are not there in front of us. When we do this, we use the information we have stored in our brains, along with our sensory memories, to add detail to our thoughts. For instance, you can imagine how an apple tastes or how it crunches when you bite into it, without actually holding an apple in your hand. Another way you can imagine is by thinking up something that still needs to be created in real life, such as changing a system or striving to achieve something—like a career move, or a creative goal or project.

Creativity requires imagining

Any invention or idea you see around you was first designed in the mind. Your imagination is your greatest creative asset; your creativity simply cannot exist without it. It's crucial, then, that you practice training your imaginative muscles, strengthening them each day.

As we saw in Chapter 5, each creative type or imaginator type thinks and designs differently. But all creatives, whatever their approach or process, draw on their imaginative capacities.

Access your imagination space

Possessing an imagination is one thing; choosing to use it is quite another. It's easy to get lazy in our thinking when we are preoccupied with everyday responsibilities and the influence of our changing environments. Sometimes we forget that we have an imagination at all, and need to get back in touch with this place where we can think differently, entertain our curiosities, and explore unknown territory.

Accessing your imagination space is easier than you think. You can begin by feeding your mind simple prompts to help unlock the door to "impossible" thoughts. Set creative constraints that spark your imagination and **give yourself permission to toss out everything you know to be true today and find the creative freedom to make fresh connections between your current mental references.**

In fast-paced work environments, there is often pressure to perform our creativity and access our imaginations "on the spot". This can be daunting and leave us feeling embarrassed if we fail to keep up with colleagues who find it easy to attack brainstorming or ideation on demand. Accessing your imagination space at a moment's notice can be tricky at first, but with practice, it will soon become second nature. If you discovered, in Chapter 5, that you are an *Idea Implementor* or *Idea Maker*, you'll especially benefit from adding practices that target this creative action point.

Expand your imagination space

Once you find it less difficult to access your imagination space, you can start to deepen your practice and strengthen your imagination muscle. At this point, you'll want to try expanding your capacity to connect the dots in your imagination space so that your mind breaks apart your conventional thinking and allows you to stretch ideas and thoughts into territories that aren't typically understood or even accepted in the here and now. This imaginative territory is where you can think up disruptive ideas, find the courage to create change, and start achieving substantial creative goals that will create a big impact or even make your wildest dreams come true.

Use the two creative challenges on the following pages to activate your imagination, generate fresh concepts, and stretch conventional thinking.

Mashups

Generate fresh concepts

Pair, or "mash up", two totally different things, using your mind's eye to strengthen your imagination muscle. Build your capacity to go beyond conventional thinking and open up space to imagine more possibilities.

Exercise these creative muscles:

Imagination
When you exercise your ability to visualise objects without the help of physical cues, you train your imagination to come up with images "on the spot".

Push creative boundaries
The practice of mashing things together in an unconventional way grows your capacity to imagine the impossible as possible without thinking twice.

How to...

1. **Start simple.** All you need for this exercise is your imagination and the making space you've chosen. Bring your creative notebook if you would like to document your ideas.
2. **Choose two things to "mash" together.** In your mind's eye, imagine two objects, places, or concepts you can combine. For example, imagine "mashing up" a high heel with an iguana, or The Rolling Stones with Mozart. Practice using only your imagination to pair two things together. This means no use of photos or physical objects.
3. **Play.** Imagine the characteristics of the two different things you chose. Use your sensory memory to explore. Play with their textures and materials. Think about the different ways you could manipulate your objects or concepts, or the different states they could inhabit. Imagine what would happen to the materials if you heated, smashed, or froze them.
4. **Mash.** Now, combine both things. Remember to merge their characteristics. How does combining them together create a new thing, idea, or concept?
5. **Give it context.** Place your new object—the "mashup"—in a fresh context. What function does your mashup have on planet Mars? How could you use it underwater or in the future?
6. **Use your notebook.** Try making sketches of your mashups. Give them titles and use them to launch stories, art projects, or new product ideas.
7. **Keep going and push boundaries.** Continue to play. If you started with a mashup of a giraffe and a toothbrush, then try combining the giraffe with something different, like a radio. What shifts? Does it become easier to create new concepts? Don't be afraid to imagine wild ideas.

Headlines from the future

Stretch conventional thinking

Imagine (im)possible futures using a simple creative storytelling technique. Travel beyond conventional ways of thinking by creating headlines from unknown futures 20+ years from now.

Exercise these creative muscles:

Imagination
By working with a not-yet-realised reality as a creative constraint, you'll train your imagination to accept the *impossible* as a *possible* form of truth.

Stretch conventional thinking
A futures-thinking practice strengthens your capacity to be original in your thinking and generate revolutionary ideas.

How to...

1. **Travel to the future.** Choose a specific year from the future and decide to travel there. Pick a year at least 20 years from now.
2. **Explore.** What do you see, feel, taste, touch, and hear? Write it down in your notebook.
3. **Imagine a future world.** Take a few moments to consider how things have changed since the present (now) in the year you've chosen. What are the new trends and driving forces? Think about science & technology, arts & culture, economics, politics, and the environment. How do living creatures behave in this future? Challenge yourself to create scenarios, characters, and objects that we can only dream of! Describe the world you imagine, write it down in your notebook, and make sketches.
4. **Choose a newsworthy topic.** Make a list of the different topics you want to explore in this future scenario. Maybe you'd like to imagine your future career, or personal life, or an issue that concerns or interests you either locally or globally (i.e. the future of water, of education, of music, or of dining). Choose just one of these ideas to work with for your headline.
5. **Pick a media channel.** Where do you want your headline to appear and who will read it? This could be a news channel, newspaper, radio, or magazine. Feel free to create a new type of media channel or technology that exists only in your future world.
6. **Write your future headline(s).** Begin writing news-style headlines. Be creative. Play with words. Imagine we live on Mars in the year 2060, and the headline reads: *Glow-in-the-dark beauty products communicate the wearer's emotions*. Or, in 2080, maybe you imagine that after the Great Flood of 2050, we hear from dolphins: *Dry land discovered near North Pole*.
7. **Enhance your stories with imagery.** Create or find an image to accompany each headline. How can you represent them visually?
8. **Share your headlines with real people in the present.** What reactions or conversations do your headlines from the future provoke? Do any ideas come out of these conversations that take you in different directions? How might you build on this type of headline, or even prevent it from actually happening?

Make

Ideas can't be fully realised until they come to life in the real, tangible world. But making isn't only about bringing ideas to life. The *make* action point helps you to break through creative blocks or to launch you into the creative process when you feel overwhelmed. Making—especially when used with the *create to create* method (Chapter 7)—can free you up to accept what your inspiration provides without judgment or pressure to perform. Making **activates your body in the creative process by opening up the channel between your thought space (or imagination) and your physical space.** This is the moment when you will begin to experience what's known as *creative flow*.

Making is an action, not a final performance

Some creative types often find making a challenge. And even those who *do* love to make can find reasons to procrastinate. Do you associate making only with creative outputs? When you're asked to *make* something, do you feel a sense of stress or pressure to perform? If this is the case, you may want to consider rethinking your definition of *making*.

While working with design professionals in global business innovation labs and design firms, I observed the crush on creativity that happened when KPIs and budgets were introduced or when executives or clients dictated the creative process, often focusing only on outputs. Understandably, organisations are designed to work towards final outcomes that will sustain their business goals. There isn't much we can do to change this fast-paced innovation cycle. Still, you can stimulate your creativity with other solutions—for example, by prioritising a personal creative practice that will fill your creative bucket and keep your creative muscles active. In this case, exercising your making muscles is not only a creativity-strengthening activity, but also a way of keeping yourself fulfilled and motivated in less-than-ideal circumstances. Return to the exercises in Chapter 2 and review what motivates you. Where can making help?

Activate your making muscles by using the following activity spread. Take the futures you designed in the previous creative challenges, and bring them to life!

"All the best ideas come out of the process; they come out of the work itself."

Chuck Close

Painter, visual artist, and photographer

Making the future

Prototyping a new reality

use this space
to create

Use this space to move what you've imagined into the real world. Take your imaginary creations from the previous exercises—*Mashups, Headlines from the future*—and practice making prototypes. Start with sketches or glue a collage into these pages.

When you are finished, take some time to reflect. *What did it feel like to channel the imagined into reality?*

Connect

Connecting our ideas to the world is just as important as imagining and making. By connecting and communicating effectively, you can link your creativity to your environment, emphasising the value of your creative contributions and the ways they impact others and the systems we live in. The *connect* creative action point highlights the importance of sharing your imagined ideas, your scrappy prototypes, and your curiosities with others throughout the process so you can elevate your creative capacities and better connect your ideas to your surroundings. Building strong connections with others relies on your ability to tell relatable and understandable stories that others can digest easily, which will help you to collaborate and ultimately bring more of your ideas to life.

Are you someone who has trouble describing your creative intentions to others? Think about how better communication might kickstart your creativity and give your ideas more reach.

Storytelling, *not story-selling*

It's common to struggle to explain all that wonderful creative thinking that goes on in your head in a way others can relate to—especially when you have invested an enormous amount of your time, energy, and emotion into a project. With so much going on inside, it's hard to know where to start in sharing your big ideas, and being too close to a project can blur your ability to explain your ideas in a compelling and comprehensible way.

When this happens, creative communication often takes a wrong turn: you go from storytelling to story-*selling*. *Storytelling* is about sharing and inviting others to connect and collaborate with your idea. Story-*selling*, on the other hand, means taking a defensive approach to explaining your idea, expecting your audience to agree with you or asking them to validate your thinking. This leads to less comfortable collaborations and feelings of defeat when others don't immediately embrace or "get" your ideas. Story-*selling* is usually a result of insecurity or unpreparedness, and it can be avoided through practice. Share your ideas frequently and take notice of how you organise your message and how it's being received. Welcome feedback and practice finding ways to communicate more clearly.

Communication as support, not judgment

Many people struggle to share their ideas, curiosities, or unfinished works because they fear being judged, criticised, or shut down. But moments of creative doubt are actually the best time to consider sharing your works in progress or your questions. When you invite others into your process early on, you can receive formative insights that you may not have arrived at while working alone. Of course, not everything in the creative process needs to be shared. An isolated process can be a creative sanctuary. But when your creativity could use a little push, hearing from others can help a lot. Don't underestimate the power of informal collaboration: you may be pleasantly surprised by the inspiring information you receive simply by opening up the conversation. A healthy debate or a different point of view can crack a good idea wide open and make it great!

Communication as meaning-making

Sharing your creative journey with others enhances your creative experience and increases confidence. It also **expands your point of view and brings shared meaning to your creative contributions**. This is important because what you design, imagine, or create, when brought to life, should contribute to its context.

Strong storytelling skills can also help you communicate your ideas and your thinking to co-creators to help push your ideas through to the next stage at work or in a team. For visionary types, learning to explain your wild ideas with clarity will bring your audience along with you when you travel to the impossible future.

I encourage you to use and practice various communication and storytelling techniques so that you can recognise the methods that best express your creative voice and find approaches that challenge you to open new channels of communication. For example, you could do storyboarding and take a visual approach to organising, mapping out, or sketching your stories. It's also a good idea to practice creative challenges that focus on delivering your ideas and developing your body confidence. Try the creative challenge *Strut your stuff* in the section at the end of the book. For now, start simple with the *Five-sentence story* on the following page.

The five-sentence story

Find your voice

Use simple creative constraints to help you focus on the message you want to deliver and the connection you want to make with your listeners. Organise your story using the magic number five—five words, five images, five sentences.

Exercise these creative muscles:

Sensemaking and clarity
When you practice limiting yourself to five, you exercise your capacity to be concise, simple, and direct so that anyone can understand you.

Connection
Getting practice with identifying which feelings you want to convey when expressing your ideas will help you to use emotions to make connections with your listeners.

How to...

1. **You have a story to tell.** Define the idea, theme, emotion, or objective you want to share with your audience. Be clear about what you are working with and write it down.

2. **Why tell it?** Reflect on your motivations for sharing and the kind of reaction you want to evoke. Is it a wild idea that people will find difficult to believe? Are you explaining how your prototype functions or improves the lives of others? Are you trying to inspire others to follow you on a journey to create an impact together?

3. **Define your audience and context.** Who needs to hear your story? Why? In what context or environment will you share your story?

4. **Now you are ready to organise your message.** Keep it simple and focus on being concise. Use the following prompts to help.

5. **Five words:** Think of five different words that describe your idea, theme, emotion, or objective.

6. **Five images:** Sketch, draw, or use existing images to expand on these five words. You can also use a five-frame storyboard to start organising your images to shape your story into a beginning, middle, and end.

7. **Five sentences:** Draw inspiration from the previous two steps and begin crafting a short, five-sentence paragraph that tells your story clearly and concisely.

8. **Deliver and test your message.** Practice sharing your five-sentence story with different people before delivering it to a larger group or important audience. Use these trial runs as a test to see if you're getting your message across. Ask for as much feedback as possible.

9. **Expand.** You can polish your five sentences so you'll always be ready to communicate your ideas. Or you could challenge yourself to expand on your short story and make a full presentation.

Reflect

Your creativity is steered by who you are and how you feel. That means it's essential to reflect on how you are, how you connect, and how you feel while creating. The *reflect* action point sets you up for intentional contemplation. Time spent thinking about how you observe the world and interact with your surroundings is time well spent. Paying attention to how you digest and make sense of stimuli, and how you express yourself in response, will help you to develop a powerful creative mindset.

A robust reflection practice also cultivates curiosity, another important creative muscle and a key part of the creative mindset. Regularly asking thought-provoking questions and seeking deep answers opens the gateway to alternative perspectives, new contexts, and different forms of understanding. Practice reflecting on how your creativity is evolving and remind yourself that you, too, are in constant evolution as you increase your creative and emotional intelligence and your ability to self-direct.

Your notebook: a creative companion
Using a notebook as a tool for reflection helps you follow your own process and allows you to use your evolving ideas as fuel for your creativity. Practice documenting thoughts, feelings, insights, and questions in real time. Capture your inspiration, self-assess your process, and **allow imperfection and messiness to occur inside the pages**. By collecting everything in one place, you'll end up with a tangible record that can be reviewed and reassessed at any time. Notice any patterns or repeated emotions across the cycle of your creative process, and don't forget to ask yourself the hard questions.

Think of your notebook as a personal assistant to your creative chaos and as a mirror that reflects your deepest creative intentions.

Find the right notebook, sketchbook, or journal. Take yourself on a creative date and go shopping for one that works for you. Think of the details and how you might use it. Do you want blank pages or lined? Hardcover or soft? Plain cover or decorated? What is the quality of the paper, and what writing utensils will you use? If you prefer to keep a digital notebook, that's okay, too, though I do recommend using at least one analogue notebook where you can play with dynamic, tangible materials.

You may decide to have separate notebooks for different creative activities. This is my approach: I designate specific notebooks to specific areas of my creative world. For example, one notebook is devoted to documenting all that happens in my daily practice, while another is used to reflect on the process of working on a single creative intention. I set up rituals for how I use the notebooks, including giving each a title, setting the time of day I will dedicate to intentional reflection, and deciding how the daily reflections will appear visually. Designing creative constraints upfront supports my long-term needs and keeps me on track with my reflective note-taking. I never have an excuse for abandoning reflection in my creative process.

My favourite part of using the notebooks is reviewing them once they are complete and highlighting important moments that happened throughout my process over time. Often, seeing my thinking methods and creation techniques laid out in front of me all at once reveals patterns, which in turn helps me discover new approaches to making and creating.

Making time to reflect

In the workplace, we are not usually offered reflection time. It is unfortunate but true. Therefore, it is up to you to insert time for reflection into your daily routine. Aim to make time for reflection every single day of your practice. Keep it simple and make a plan to write down two sentences in your notebook twice a day, once in the morning and also at the end of the day. Include the emotions you felt while creating (or *not* creating) and the moments where you were challenged in the process, or pleasantly surprised or delighted by the unexpected.

For managers or design leaders, a reflection notebook can be an excellent tool for noticing patterns in the way your team is delivering creative projects. Reviewing your notebook at the end of a project is an effective way to discover how you can improve your leadership skills and how to have open conversations with your team about collaboration before starting the next project.

Reflect

Make space

use this space
to create

Use the space below to practice activating your capacity to reflect. Start by setting a timer for 5–10 minutes. You can use the following prompts to kickstart your reflection period or create your own thought-provoking questions for contemplation.

Which of the creative action points need the most exercise? Why? What scares or excites you most about attempting to activate your ability to *imagine, make, connect, or reflect*? Write down any insights, emotions, thoughts, or ideas that come up throughout the reflection process.

Chapter 10
Your creative roadmap

Set clear intentions and measure your progress

"

In the creative act, the artist goes from intention to realisation through a chain of totally subjective reactions. His struggle toward the realisation is a series of efforts, pains, satisfaction, refusals, decisions, which also cannot and must not be fully self-conscious, at least on the esthetic plane.

Marcel Duchamp
Painter, sculptor, writer, and pioneer of the DADA movement

By now, you've likely learned that the journey through creativity is long, beautiful, and demanding. What you set out to do isn't always where you end up—and no matter which direction you take your creativity, you can be certain you'll face the struggle.

Creative struggle may be unavoidable, but, as we've discovered, it can be managed—and even harnessed as a powerful form of inspiration.

If you've worked your way through the previous chapters, you now have all the tools you need to move forward with your next creative endeavour. There is truly nothing that can stand in your way. In the next stage, you'll work on identifying where you want to venture next—and begin!

But first, let's review your creative journey and the toolbox you've developed using this book. Check off the exercises you completed—and feel proud of yourself! If you've missed out on any chapters, now is a great time to go back and fill in the gaps.

Here's what you've learned so far:

- ☐ Ch. 1: You created a unique definition of creativity—*Creativity is* **You**
- ☐ Ch. 2: You got to know your motivations for creating—*Why? Why not?*
- ☐ Ch. 3: You learned about accepting yourself for who and where you are today —*Start from where you are.*
- ☐ Ch. 4: You started to understand the environment around your creativity —*Context matters.*
- ☐ Ch. 5: You identified your imaginator type—*Idea Generator, Idea Maker, Idea Implementer.*
- ☐ Ch. 6: You befriended your creative struggle(s)—*Embracing the tension.*
- ☐ Ch. 7: You defined your creative practice to fit your life—*Building creative habits.*
- ☐ Ch. 8: You designed your active creation space(s)—*Exploring places and objects.*
- ☐ Ch. 9: You exercised your creative action points—*Imagine. Make. Connect. Reflect.*
- ☑ **Well done!**

Hopefully, you're now feeling the momentum and understanding more about your creative potential and the impact you can make by committing yourself to making and sharing your creative contributions with the world. Let this momentum be the creative spark you've needed—or longed for. Use it to **pull yourself out of procrastination mode and launch yourself into the creative life you envision.**

What have you dreamed of doing but haven't yet started? Do you have a wild idea that keeps you awake at night? Is there a wicked problem out there begging for you to solve it?

Now is the time to identify new projects—but also to be deliberate about how you want to spend your creative energy. Instead of tackling every creative goal or dream at once, **set clear creative intentions and outline a roadmap to follow.** Working with a creative outline will not only keep you on track, it will also help you observe and measure your progress along the way and guide you on when to make a U-turn, when to stop and course-correct, and when to push through your struggle and keep going.

Building a creative roadmap is a way of setting clear expectations for yourself. If you're someone who has trouble following through on projects you start, you'll find that the roadmap is an exceptional creative tool capable of supporting you all the way through to the finish line.

Let's start working through the steps that will help you create your roadmap.

Clear the noise

One of the common worries I hear from creatives struggling to move forward is that they don't know how to choose a project from the plethora of things they want to work on or the variety of talents they'd like to exercise. This state of stress around choosing the "right" thing to tackle is paralyzing. When you feel anxious about abandoning one creative "baby" for another, you may start to experience physical cues like an ache in your heart or a queasy flip-flop in your stomach. It somehow feels wrong to give up a "great" creative idea or goal and focus on something else.

You may not realise it in this state, but you can do it all—just not all of it *right now*. But if you stall your decision-making process, and fail to choose at all, you will end up in a state of yearning, the worst sort of creative limbo. This will send you walking on the uneventful and dissatisfying path of procrastination.

So how do you choose?

This is where creative tools come in to assist with the overwhelming decision-making process. One of my favourites is the **Brain dump**, a simple yet powerful exercise that will let you clear the noise and sift through unwanted distractions. Doing a *Brain dump* will free up your mental space so you can home in on the creative intentions that matter to you most.

Start removing distractions by doing a *Brain dump* on the following page. Then return to the checklist below to practice narrowing down your choices.

Practice choosing one creative goal at a time
Once you've cleared away the unnecessary intruders squatting in your mental space, you can start to consider which one creative desire most deeply resonates with you at present. This is the one you will prioritize.

Reflect on what makes this creative urge or ambition so important to you right now. Return to the creative toolbox you developed in Part 1 of this book to understand the context.

Use this checklist to help. Ask yourself:
- [ ] What about this creative desire motivates me?
- [ ] What was holding me back before?
- [ ] How can I reframe any perceived limitations, using a *why **not** me?/why **not** now?* attitude?
- [ ] What does the "box" I've defined look like?
- [ ] How will my superpowers, vulnerabilities, and imaginator type support me?
- [ ] Where might I struggle? What do I need to explore or learn to carry out this project?

The first time you go through this process, it may take some time. But the more you practice using the *Brain dump* followed by this quick check-in, the quicker and better you'll be able to value your creative options and navigate the decision-making phase with ease.

After you've finished your *Brain dump*, continue to page 102 for the next step in developing your creative roadmap.

Brain dump

Remove distractions and prioritise
meaningful creation

use this space
to create

Remove the clutter from your thought space so you can eliminate distractions and focus on creative intentions that matter. Get a sheet of paper and writing utensils and prepare to "dump" everything that's in your brain onto the paper. Write or sketch whatever comes up: emotions, aspirations, concerns, tasks, responsibilities, dreams, ideas, etc. Once you've finished, take a look! What do you see? Are there any patterns? Now circle or highlight anything that resonates with you or jumps out of the page. Take a few moments to sit with your *Brain dump* and reflect. What matters most? Now return to page 99.

Make it tangible. Write it down.

Getting your creative intentions down on paper is the first step to bringing them **out of your head and into reality**. Start by taking a few moments to reflect on the intention you've chosen to work with (for now), and use specific words to describe it clearly and meaningfully as it relates to you.

If it helps, you can begin with a statement like this:

"I want to _____ because _____ ".
Or
"I need to _____ because _____ ".

This will help you both identify a clear objective and understand the personal motivation that drives it.

WRITE YOUR CREATIVE INTENTION HERE:

Writing down your objective gives it life. Posting it somewhere in clear view reminds you that it requires your attention and action. I like to write my creative intention on a post-it and hang it up on the whiteboard behind my desk. I also dedicate a sketchbook or journal to the process. I give the notebook a title and set a time for daily reflection on my intention. Remember, objects can be your creative companions.

Design a roadmap

Many people have experience designing strategies in their professional lives, but don't think of using strategic design principles for their own creative projects and goals. A practical way to begin is to **draw out a simple map that provides you with a snapshot of your potential creative journey**. Think of this creative roadmap as a flexible tool rather than a fixed one. On your map, you will *start from where you are* and use your creative intention statement to direct you toward what you are aiming to achieve. To keep it simple you can mark these two points and then connect them with a line. At the starting point you can write out your current desires, strengths, limitations, and resources. Then, lay out the territories you would like to visit on the journey toward your creative destination.

Set milestones to measure your progress

Assign milestones to act as stops along the way where you can check in with yourself and manage your expectations and progress. For example, you could attach a timeline to the "territories" or pitstops you identified in mapping out your journey—though you should make sure to leave room for things to shift and change along the way. You could also set key milestones associated with different phases of your project. For example, if your creative intention is to publish a blog, you could use these milestones:

Milestone 1: Reviewed 20 comparable blogs as research (one-month mark)
Milestone 2: Set up blog platform (two-month mark)
Milestone 3: Wrote first three blog posts (three-month mark)
...and so on.

Be as specific as you feel is necessary and remember to be realistic and honest with what is feasible.

Setting creative milestones can help you stay motivated during the creative process. This will help you keep a pulse on any urge that may arise to focus on unnecessary distractions, find excuses to procrastinate, or abandon the path entirely.

These markers of projected progress are not intended to be pressure points you *must reach by a certain time*, but rather check-in points that will guide you back to your main focus, especially in moments of doubt or low motivation. The creative way is never a straight path—it demands that you adapt to the unexpected. Use your milestones to understand your progress and remind yourself of your original plans. Then, see what needs adapting, make the change, and move on.

Use the space in the following activity spread to draw your creative roadmap.
Work through the checklist below to guide your reflections as you decide how you will approach your creative objective. Use the creative toolbox you developed in Part 2 of this book to set yourself up for a successful journey, while keeping in mind what you've learned about designing effective creative spaces and practice methods.

Use this checklist to help:

- [ ] How will I set up my creative practice to achieve this goal?
  - [ ] Style or approach
  - [ ] Time
  - [ ] Space
- [ ] How will I utilise my creative action points throughout the process?
  - [ ] Imagine
  - [ ] Make
  - [ ] Connect
  - [ ] Reflect

Plan for success
Commit to following through right from the start. Plan to do only what you can actually manage for both long-term and short-term plans. If thinking about the big picture long-term sends you into a spiral, begin by breaking the process down into smaller pieces. Instead of thinking about how to get to where you're going across one whole year, break the year down into 52 weeks and set small, achievable goals and milestones for each. Fifty-two weeks: that means **52 opportunities to make creative choices** and 52 chances to act on the creative intentions you set for yourself over the course of one year. If you approach your creative practice week by week, you will also experience 52 reasons to celebrate the transformation of your creativity.

Lean in. Let it go. Let it flow.

You will visit many places during your creative journey, from the initial stage of observation and wonder, to questioning your curiosity, to the moment inspiration strikes. Some of those destinations will feel very comfortable to you as you explore and experiment, while others will feel less comfortable or even unbearable.

Lean into **this discomfort.**

There is always a certain level of uncertainty when you enter the creative process. You may think you know where you would like to direct your creativity, but if you rigidly fixate on your destination, you'll miss out on other unexpected sources of inspiration along the way that can elevate your ideas to their fullest potential. Put your trust and faith in the process. A flexible creative roadmap will teach you the hard lessons and provide you with all you require to work through the struggle, while leading you where you need to be.

Don't forget to take these creative principles with you on the road:
- Creativity is for always. Make time and space for your creative intentions.
- Start from where you are. You are ready to begin right now.
- Show up no matter what. To *be* creative, you have to *do* creative.
- Take small bites out of the process. Keep it simple.
- Share with others and make connections. Practice story*telling.*
- Forget about outcomes. Embrace the process.
- Take time to reflect. Use your notebook to document insights and inspirations.
- Celebrate yourself and acknowledge your creativity. Do it often!

Surviving creative road bumps

In the final part of this book, we will address common road bumps and potholes found on the road to creative bliss and practical tools and tips to move past them.

Creative roadmap

Your guided journey to making

use this space
to create

Draw out a simple map of your potential creative journey toward a particular goal or intention. Start with a line that connects where you are starting today with where you are headed. At the starting point, write out your current desires, strengths, limitations, and resources. Then, lay out all the different territories you hope to visit on the journey towards your creative destination. Set milestones to measure your progress. Remember to revisit your roadmap during the process and adapt it when necessary.

Part 3:

Maintaining your creative momentum

So now what?
Don't stop—keep on making!

If you've been exercising your creativity muscles using Parts 1 and 2 of this book, you should be starting to feel the power and freedom of your creative momentum. You may be asking yourself:

How do I maintain this sense of creative ease?
How can I be sure I won't fall into procrastination mode once again?

You may also be wondering how you'll overcome new challenges like creative burnout, creative blocks, and the noise of everyday distractions.

This section will show you how to fuel your creative momentum no matter what life throws at you. As we all know, motivation can fade. Challenges during the creative struggle can trigger your old patterns and send you back into procrastination mode. But there's no need to panic or allow doubt to creep in. This section will guide you through key techniques for maintaining a robust and healthy creative practice that will keep your making energy flowing—and provide you with straightforward solutions to pick yourself up when you've lost your momentum. With these tips and tricks, you'll learn how to stay connected to your motivations for creating and bounce back from challenges, stronger and more satisfied than before!

And finally, as a friendly reminder that living a creative life means the work is never done, in this last section, you will be dared to "level up". It's time to learn how to take your creative courage into the next challenge and build momentum you never thought possible. Let's get started!

Chapter 11
Creative momentum

What to do when you lose your spark

> **"**
> *With the combination of consistency, progress, and motivation you achieve momentum. You go from being an immovable object to an unstoppable force.*

Srinivas Rao
Author and founder of *The Unmistakable Creative* podcast

Creative momentum is what every maker and artist is searching for. And momentum isn't just something we creative types *want*—it's something we *need* to bring our ideas to life and allow our creativity to flourish.

Also known as "*creative flow*" or "*the zone*", momentum happens when your creative actions feed one another and you feel a sense of energy and ease in the process of making. With momentum, motivation comes easily and your ideas are fluid and generative. Time no longer exists when you are in *flow*; you enter a state of pure creative freedom. Gaining creative momentum is exciting and inspiring.

But what happens when you lose your momentum?

Losing momentum is painful
Feeling your momentum slipping away can leave you creatively paralysed. Often, when we lose

our flow, feelings of failure can start to bubble up and the fear that we've wasted time building creative energy only to see it disappear can send us reeling. In these moments, you may worry that you've lost your creative capacities altogether, or, worse, that inspiration has decided to abandon you—for good. Don't panic. Just remember, in times like these, **your creativity is *always* with you**. It just needs the right kind of attention.

So what can you do to rebuild the forward motion of momentum?

Take a deep breath and move on

Remember to *start from where you are* and focus on taking that small, first step back to creativity. Choose to pick yourself up and begin again from wherever you are. Don't judge yourself for falling out of the rhythm you had going. There's no need to get stuck focusing on what happened and why you lost it.

Next, start again. With *anything*. Keep doing it. Do more of it. Continue until you recover your creative mojo. Show up no matter what.

When you feel awkward, uninspired, or overwhelmed, it's difficult to imagine yourself in the flow of your creativity and know where to begin. It's at times like this you need to remember **you've done it before and you can do it again.**

Don't expect to start "in the zone"

Building your momentum is a slow, step-by-step process. What's more, you'll usually find yourself starting from a standstill, or, at best, restarting after a halt in your creative process. This can be tough, and the stress of starting from nothing can send many of us straight into procrastination mode. It's best, in these moments, not to focus on the endgame or think about how far you have to go. Instead, look to the immediate task in front of you. Every baby step you take, every challenge you overcome, and every uninspiring moment you wriggle your way through is powerful when you're trying to (re) gain momentum. The click will happen, I promise. For some, that magic moment will occur after a few consecutive days of practice, while others might take weeks or months to hit their stride. Remind yourself that this isn't a race to the finish line. Building momentum is about keeping the energy alive throughout the whole process.

Trust the process

Creative momentum is magical. When I find myself *in the zone*, I feel unstoppable. Ideas are flowing, inspiration is around every corner, and sometimes I can't turn off the stream of delightful obsessions that call to me from the creative wormholes of my mind. And, honestly, I don't *want* to turn it off. With creative momentum behind me, I feel alive, happy, and motivated. In this space, all is possible. This momentum is the reward for my dedication and commitment, for all the time and energy I've invested in my creativity.

Have you ever felt this? If so, you're probably hoping to return to this feeling—and you can.

When the light has dimmed on your flow, **trusting the process is everything**. By working through this book, you'll have started to understand how your unique creative process works. Believe in it and it will provide you with all that you need, through every twist and unforeseen turn.

Just keep going

In times when I lose that exhilarating momentum, I begin to feel blue and unmotivated. Instead of unstoppable, I feel my creativity is *impossible*. Many creatives experience moments of darkness or even depression that can make getting back on track a struggle. This is when you need your creativity even more than it needs you. This is the time to get in there and start making—no matter what!

Often, losing your momentum is a result of life's many distractions, such as shifts in schedule, work pressure, everyday household tasks, or the expectations of others. It's easy to unravel when you give your power away or put your energy into places outside of your creative focus. But never forget that you are capable and deserve to have the time and space for creative fulfilment. **Never underestimate the power of your own creativity.**

While writing this book, I held a useful phrase close to help me work through the creative struggle: *starve distractions, feed the focus*. I repeated this phrase when the process got sticky; overwhelming, or just plain exhausting. Having mantras or "power phrases" to draw on during the process can keep you motivated and give you that extra support you need when it's just you and the work.

The plain truth is that life's responsibilities and unexpected twists can't be avoided or controlled. What you *can* control is how you handle them. Distractions will try to steal your focus, but don't give in. Deal with challenges head on and find ways to incorporate life into your creative process.

Prioritise, don't (over)dramatise
Emotions follow us on the creative journey—and sometimes, they even drive it. Learning how to connect with and manage your emotions will serve your creativity. "Managing" your emotions doesn't mean pushing your feelings away, but rather the opposite. When life happens, take the time to feel all your feelings. You can even use them in your creativity. But **save the drama for the stage**. Don't let complicated feelings and situations control you. When things get difficult, take a step back to assess what's happening and reassess your plans, and then prioritise the next best move. Revisit your creative roadmap from Chapter 10 as a guide.

That means when you feel blue, you should stop to feel it—and then move on. My late grandma had a wonderful saying. She said, "Holly, it's okay to get on the pity pot from time to time, but you must also know when to get up and move on." Grandma B was a strong and vivacious woman who knew what she was talking about.

Set yourself up for the marathon
Meaningful creative work usually means a long process—maybe even a forever process. Even when a project comes to an end, it doesn't mean your work is done. If you want to keep the momentum going, you'll have to continue putting energy and effort into your creativity—always.

Remember: your momentum won't be at the same level all the time. It's natural for your motivation to ebb and flow. With practice, you will become a pro at managing the highs and lows of your creative process and finding unique ways to direct your energy and get back in the zone.

Use the following page to get your creativity back on track. Commit to a 30-day challenge to start building back your momentum.

Your 30-day challenge

Build momentum

1	2	3
7	8	9
13	14	15
19	20	21
25	26	27

Commit to a 30-day creative challenge of your choice. Use the 30 spaces below to log your process. Put a mark in each space to celebrate your commitment to show up for your creativity. Keep a reflection notebook during the process. At the end of 30 consecutive days of practice, consider how you experienced creative momentum. Did you feel that "magic moment" of flow kick in? When did it happen? What emotions came up?

4	5	6
10	11	12
16	17	18
22	23	24
28	29	30

Chapter 12
Reframe creative blocks

Empower yourself to shift the circumstances

>
> *The power of mistakes enables us to reframe creative blocks and turn them around...*
> *The troublesome parts of our work, the parts that are most baffling and frustrating, are in fact the growing edges. We see these opportunities the instant we drop our preconceptions and our self-importance.*

Stephen Nachmanovitch
Musician, author, computer artist, and educator

As we know, the long, complex journey to achieving your creative goals comes with a few roadblocks along the way. These barriers to making—known as "creative blocks"—are inevitable, and creatives of every level experience them at some point. But there's no need to sweat it. You can build the resilience you need to overcome these painful disruptions to your process again and again. A change in attitude and a new way of approaching creative blocks will allow you to shift your circumstances and keep on making.

Firstly, understand that blocks are always temporary and that they will eventually release themselves into new energy. Sometimes, feeling stuck or uninspired can have a purpose: to force you to move in a different direction. Secondly, remember that **what you perceive as a "block" may actually be the whisper of inspiration**. It all depends on how you view it and how you choose to react. Finally, remind yourself that the sooner you get comfortable with the feelings of discomfort that these awkward barriers bring up, the easier it will be to work through your blocks and all the frustration they generate.

So how can you identify a creative block?

Two types of creative blocks

There are two main kinds of creative barriers: those that stem from circumstances beyond your control, and those you create for yourself. Ask yourself which type of creative block you are facing before unleashing your emotions.

Type 1: Roadblocks created by others

These include:

- Systems that make it challenging to move forward
- Others' attitudes or expectations

You may not be able to change or remove roadblocks that emerge because of others, but you do have the power to choose how you react to them—and to create clever workarounds. Use your creative toolbox to open new channels and unlock underutilised resources. You could start by revisiting Chapter 4 to understand more about the context that surrounds you and home in on which aspects of your environment are disrupting your creative flow. Is there an opportunity to shift your thinking about a perceived limitation? Would acquiring more knowledge about the system or its rules help you overcome the block?

The people you collaborate with can be a common source of creative block. Think back to what you learned about the different imaginator types in Chapter 5, and consider how your co-creators think and *make* best. How could you improve your collaboration with others to include everyone's super strengths and vulnerabilities? Accept that others will have their own ways of working, and know that what they think or say does not define who you are or your work.

Type 2: Creative barriers created by you

Common self-generated blocks include:
- Fear of starting or moving forward
- Unsupportive mental narratives about yourself and your creativity
- Lack of dedication, commitment, or willingness to put in the work

Once you realise that certain negative circumstances are the result of your own behaviours or thinking, you can start to understand that you also have the power to change them. Face your fears through a combination of reflection and action. Rewrite old narratives that no longer support you. Step up for yourself and commit to doing the work.

Again, review the exercises in Parts 1 and 2 of this book. These will help you to understand where you're getting in your own way and what you need to change. Perhaps your motivation has changed since starting a project, or something in how you are approaching your creative practice isn't working and needs revising. Check in with your creative roadmap (you may want to go back to Chapter 10 for a refresher on building and updating your roadmap). Consider whether your creative block is happening because you are fixating on the endgame instead of adapting to the process.

The creative blocks you make for yourself can be the most challenging to work through, mainly because they usually originate in old, firmly-entrenched patterns or habits that no longer serve your creativity. Relax, and don't stress. No one is asking you to change all at once—or to change at all—but it may be time to realise that things could be different and to start imagining what that would look like!

Creative blocks can be good

Creative blocks. ugh. We all know that feeling when nothing seems to click, and you want to give up... *but you can't.* Every single one of us will experience closed channels blocking our creative capacities at some stage of the process.

So, then—
*If creative blocks are an inevitable part of the creative process, then **why can't they be used as a positive source of creative energy?***

What you usually interpret as a no-access point blocking your creativity is really a precautionary warning sign, reminding you not to get too comfortable relying on the same methods or creative capacities. These temporary creative detours are your body's way of guiding you toward new channels of creativity that can push you to expand yourself and achieve what you are truly capable of.

Complacency and stagnation are the death of creativity. The true purpose of a creative block is not to stop your creative flow, but instead to drive your creative process to change for the better.

When a lack of inspiration strikes, especially when you need it most, it is usually accompanied by feelings of frustration and panic. Your inner voice screams, "Oh, no!" and you hold on tightly to the limitations in front of you and resist change. It is this resistance that obstructs positive opportunities for creative change, *not the block itself.*

When you find yourself in a staredown with an ugly creative block, take a long deep breath and pay close attention to what it is trying to tell you. Listen closely to your creative intuition and collaborate with what's blocking you, for it always knows best, and will guide you toward different possibilities.

A new attitude
Practice shifting your attitude. Turn feelings of frustration into states of curiosity and possibility. Reframe the narrative: instead of thinking "Oh no, a creative block!", tell yourself a more positive story—"Oh yes, at last, a creative block!"

This simple rephrase can get you to entirely rethink how you view creative blocks and open up unexpected gateways to your full potential and flow. A truly creative attitude embraces all of your emotions, including frustration, and says, "That's cool; we can work with this. Let's go." Frustration is driven by expectations, and expectations make fortune-tellers of us all as we try to control what will happen. But we cannot know what tomorrow brings— which means there is no reason to force ourselves into tiny boxes based on what we once imagined or hoped for, without understanding that **there are more options.**

It's okay to quit

There is one last block to consider—and it is a dangerous one, because, if not addressed, it can turn into a cement wall and have lasting effects on your creative health. This tricky block is the one that happens when you try to force yourself to finish something even though all odds are against you or the project.

I have met this beast a few times, and the best decision I made in these cases was to quit. Yes, I said it, *quit...* give up, throw in the towel, forget about it—you get the idea. Saying goodbye to months of hard work and the money and time you've spent is more than difficult; it's excruciating. This is a struggle very few want to face, but it, too, is inescapable on the journey to creative truth and freedom.

There is nothing wrong with abandoning an idea, a project, or a creative relationship that is not working. Consider it your creative responsibility to throw out things that will suck your creativity dry and steal the imaginative energy you can better utilize elsewhere. When you find yourself making the final decision to pull the plug on a lost-cause project, take a moment to fully recognise the effort you and your co-creators have put in—and then move on. Use your notebook to reflect on what did or did not work, and take these insights with you to the next project. Saying goodbye is never easy, but once you recognise that the block is impassable and move on, you will find a glimmer of that original project somewhere else—where it was meant to be.

The best cure for creative blocks, of course, is to **start making!**

Use the exercise on the following page to move blocked energy elsewhere and shift your creative state.

"Another word for creativity is courage."

Henri Matisse

Painter, printmaker, and sculptor

Make emotions

Feel with your hands

Play with clay to explore, release, and transform the emotions that are connected to your creativity. Use the act of making as a way to break through creative blocks.

Exercise these creative muscles:

Making
Taking physical action in any form helps move ideas, energy, and emotions through your creative flow.

Emotional intelligence
The practice of paying closer attention to your emotions and incorporating them into the creative process brings you closer to understanding who you are, what motivates you, how you react to others, and how you interact with the influences of your surroundings.

How to...

1. **Prepare your materials and making space.** Clear a table or desk to create room for making. Get yourself some clay. You don't need to go out and purchase every colour—begin with one shade or choose the primary colours (you can always mix!).

2. **Get in the making mood.** Play some music or create quiet time away from outside influences. Take a brief moment to reflect on any emotions you may be feeling.

3. **Don't think, *make*.** Forget planning what you are going to create. Just start using your hands. Let your creative process and your body's interactions with the clay call your emotions to the table. Listen. Be attentive to what your hands are doing.

4. **Play.** Roll it. Squish it. Throw it against the table, the floor, or the wall. Let the actions of your hands as they work with the clay speak for you and express your emotions.

5. **Work it into something.** Once you have spent some time getting acquainted with the material and have allowed your hand movements to speak, begin making your "final" creation(s).

6. **Consider reworking it.** Clay is flexible. Practice reshaping your creations to reflect the changes you feel in your emotional state during the process of creation.

Chapter 13
Creative intermissions

Rest, rejoice, reboot

"

Almost everything will work again if you unplug it for a few minutes, including you.

Anne Lamott
Novelist and non-fiction writer

It takes continued effort to build your creative momentum, and that exertion can be both thrilling and exhausting. These intense feelings are the body's way of keeping a pulse on your staying power. Exhaustion is there to let you know when it's time to take a pause.

Creative intermissions don't mean putting the brakes on the momentum you have built up. Instead, they ask you to shift your energy momentarily so that you can continue when you're ready. This is a chance to rest, rejoice, and reboot.

Taking a time-out from your daily routine or a particular project is healthy for the evolution of your ideas, and lets you actively acknowledge your making habits. Resting is an opportunity to relax into the creative energy you have worked so hard to generate while also rejoicing in what you are building. Spending time resting, reflecting, and celebrating the impact of your creative contributions is a marvellous way to keep yourself and others motivated during the making process.

Sometimes, though, the creative struggle is so intense you just need a full reboot that will let you shut off a difficult project completely and temporarily turn your focus towards something unrelated to re-energise you and restore your creative vitality.

Experienced practitioners swear by **creative intermissions as a surefire way to stay connected to their inspiration and keep their creative momentum going.** Most say that it is during these recesses that inspiration finds its way to their doorstep. Many creative types have talked about how walks in nature help them to boost their creativity and access the imagination space. Follow their lead and try using the exercise at the end of this chapter to guide you on a nature excursion of your own and awaken your sense of awe.

Remember: your creativity needs a break, too. In the same way that you're working to exercise your creativity, your creativity is working just as hard for *you*. Making a return on your creative investment requires new inputs that can only be found when you step away from the action and allow some breathing room for the work to simply dry, settle in, or blossom.

Resist the push to *be* creative; go out and *feel* creative.
Sometimes the desire to grow your creative capacities, or the pressure to keep the energy alive on a project, can lead you to miss the joy of your creative process. With all the effort and exertion, you may forget to *live* the creative adventure. Losing yourself in the act of inventing can also make you forget how to connect to the world around you.

When you reach this point, I encourage you to step back from your daily push to *be* creative and go out and *feel* creative. Enjoy the adventures that will feed the creative beast and bring it back to life.

So, where to begin? Here's where to start:

Take it easy and daydream
Watch the clouds roll by and get lost in your imagination. Give yourself time to **be distracted by the wonderful small moments that bring you joy.** Whether you use daydreaming as an escape or a way of imagining wonderful impossibilities, it is a great use of a creative intermission. Daring to dream is pure creative freedom.

A creative love affair
Taking your creativity out on the town is an excellent way to remind yourself of the unique interests and desires that make your creativity so special. You are your own inspiration. Choose a specific time of the week to go on a "date" with your creativity, and plan an adventure that nourishes your soul. Allow yourself to relax into the experience and enjoy what you feel and discover. The best creative love affairs open doors to important emotions that remind you that you are alive!

Follow these simple steps:
- Set a time and place for the creative adventure (and don't cancel on yourself!)
- Do something that brings you joy—and do it with no other purpose than to enjoy yourself
- Explore something new, and let your curiosity take the lead

Get started with these inspiring locations and activities:
- Go to museums, exhibitions, and libraries
- Visit playgrounds, parks, or beaches
- Play like a child again—make sidewalk chalk drawings
- Take nature or city walks
- Go dancing, hiking, or biking
- Take a class on something new
- Peruse antique shops, record collections, and used bookstores
- Visit pet stores, the zoo, or a farm
- Get lost in art supplies stores and play with new tools
- Try new foods & flavours

Bring home a souvenir

While on your creative adventure, look for an object—or create one—that you can bring back to your making space (you can revisit Chapter 8 for a reminder of how to design this space). Use simple objects in your creative space as positive reminders of your experiences and as sources of inspiration. For example, bring back a rock you found on your nature walk or a new colourful pen from the art supplies store. Snap a photo you can frame or hang next to your making space.

Acknowledge and celebrate yourself

Admiring your work is a necessary part of the creative process. Your *creative intermission* should honour and respect your daily creative work. Stopping to recognise all of the ups and downs that you've endured along the way can motivate you to pick up the work again and carry on. Go ahead—throw your arms up in the air, wear that gorgeous smile, and celebrate yourself!

Make time to:
- Put down the "work" and applaud, appreciate, and respect what you are creating
- Feel good... and really *feel* it!
- Give yourself a high five or bust out a joyful dance move (don't just imagine it, really do it!)

Make time for restoration

Don't let the pressure of project deadlines or other responsibilities lead you to believe you don't have time for a creative intermission. Your creative process *needs* you to make room to rest, rejoice, and reboot. A well-used break, even a small one, is sometimes all you need to restore your sense of momentum and creative confidence.

If for no other reason, gift yourself a creative intermission as a reminder to **be kind to yourself and enjoy the process.**

Nature as inspiration

Awaken your sense of awe

Use time spent with nature as a *creative intermission* to grow your curiosity and find inspiration.

Exercise these creative muscles:

Opening your senses
When you practice listening and looking with intention, you open up your senses and connect to sources of inspiration surrounding you that you might not have noticed.

Uncertainty and curiosity
When you exercise your ability to investigate things that interest you or things you know little about, you train yourself to be comfortable navigating unknown territory.

How to...

1. **Set aside time to connect with nature.** Find at least 15 minutes in your day to meet with nature. Approach this exercise with a sense of calm. It's better not to rush.
2. **Choose a place to spend your nature time.** Take a walk. Lay in the grass. Sit on the beach. You decide.
3. **Set an intention.** Before you head out on your nature date, decide on an intention or design an activity you can do while in nature. For example, plan to collect leaves, build a tower of rocks, observe an animal in its habitat, or watch the clouds passing by. Or you can decide to simply invite your curiosity along and let it lead the way.
4. **Time to meet up with nature.** Use your intention to get you started with your nature time—and then allow nature to surprise you with its own plans.
5. **Stop, pause, and be present.** Give yourself moments of awareness to take it all in. Remember to use all of your senses.
6. **Reflect, wonder, and question.** Allow the experience to pique your curiosity or help you to see the world around you (and the world inside of you!) from a new perspective. Do you feel a sense of awe? Has it sparked a new appreciation for your environment? How?
7. **Document it.** Use a notebook and/or camera to document the experience.
8. **Take nature home with you.** Gather leaves, plants, rocks, or sticks. Then use them to make a sculpture or a collage. Use your sense of awe as inspiration. Write a poem or a short story that describes your feelings about what you experienced.
9. **Reflect.** How has your relationship with nature shifted your creative process? How might you use any aspect of your experience to launch a new idea or create something?

Chapter 14
Creative courage

Dare to level up

"

What would life be
if we had no courage
to attempt anything?

Vincent van Gogh
Post-impressionist painter

Not everyone has the guts to follow their creative urges and learn how to be creative... but I have a strong feeling *you* do. Otherwise, you wouldn't have picked up this book. Without curiosity and courage, you certainly wouldn't have made it this far. This may be the end of this book, but it's only the beginning of your next creative chapter.

You are brave, creative, and committed, and I see you.

You have already proven that the creative struggle is a beast you can manage—in fact, it's a beautiful beast you can look straight in the eye and find ways to work with.

I am proud of you, and you should be, too.

Stay courageous and dare to level up
A satisfying creative life involves deliberately choosing to invite the struggle in again and

again, welcoming the challenges it brings while celebrating its gifts. The more you practice, the more creatively confident and comfortable you will become. But there is one last hurdle you must overcome—and that is **knowing when it's time to level up.**

You'll experience times when you need to move on from the cosy and comfortable places you have carved out for your creativity and move up to the next level. This may be intimidating or even scary, as you realise you are a beginner once more in this new stage. You may find yourself asking, "What if I get it wrong?", "What if I'm not good enough?", "What if I make a fool of myself?", "What if... ?" **These *what-ifs* can immobilise your creative process... if you let them.** So *don't*.

Imagine this! *What if...* it all goes well? *What if* it is enjoyable? *What if* you grow from it?

What if the world missed out on what you have to offer?

The next chapter is yours to write
Be courageous and go where you have never gone before. The positive *what-ifs* are waiting for you there. Creative courage is daring yourself to face the things that frighten you, and making the decision every single day to put in the effort to evolve your ideas and advance your intentions. You can write your own story. The world is waiting to receive your unique contributions. All you have to do is *start making.*

Use your creative toolbox
Effective, healthy creative practices require support. **You're not meant to create alone.** Review the tools you've gained throughout this book to guide you through the rough spots. Engage creative partners in the process by co-creating with different imaginator types. Revisit or rebuild your creative roadmap, and remember your finest creative companion: your notebook.

You have everything you need to put procrastination behind you once and for all and live your creative dreams. You only have to start from where you are, put in the practice, and keep on making.

Be brave and begin. I dare you!

Part 4:

More ways to make

Grow your creative capacities

How did you get here?

You may have turned directly to this section without completing the other chapters first. That's fine; I don't mind. You're curious, and that's terrific. You want to get to work and start making—fantastic! I'm proud of you for starting.

Or maybe you're reaching this section because you committed to the journey chapter by chapter—in which case, "bravo!" I would like to congratulate you, and offer you this section as your reward—a chance for more making.

However you ended up here, I welcome you to enjoy this series of creative challenges to help strengthen and train your creative muscles and ignite your creative action points so you can better *imagine*, *make*, *connect*, and *reflect*.

How to use these pages
Choose one creative challenge to work on for seven consecutive days (or make this a 30-day challenge). Note that each challenge points out the creative muscles you'll target—from curiosity, reinvention, and storytelling, to body confidence, prototyping, decision-making, stretching the imagination, working with creative constraints, and more...

A good approach to tackling the challenges is the "repeated technique" method explained in Chapter 7: the main objective is to repeat an exercise over and over, or work through a challenge every day over time, so as to build creative strength. Remember to be intentional about how you use time and space to activate your creative capacities—take a look back at Chapter 8 if you need a refresher.

Practice alone or in groups or teams
Whether you need additional creative support or you want to help develop others' creativity, you'll find that all of the creative challenges included in this book can be used in groups. This is great for team leaders, managers, teachers, or anyone trying to cultivate an environment that supports a creative mindset or culture. Work with your chosen group in the same way you practice showing up for the challenges alone. Make sure you give the group time and space each day to repeat. Then watch the creative momentum and motivation build!

The possibilities for making are endless. Think of these creative challenges as a launching pad or a deeper look into what you are fully capable of.

Strut your stuff

Use body language and movement to express yourself

Your body is one of your most valuable creative tools. Identify and practice the body language you use to express yourself and your ideas. Grow comfortable with the movements that represent you.

Exercise these creative muscles:

Body confidence
When you practice exploring movements that you find uncomfortable, as well as those that feel comfortable, you naturally become more self-assured in how you use your unique body.

Storytelling
When you practice connecting your movement to your emotions, you increase your capacity to express yourself openly and honestly.

How to...

1. **Create space.** Locate a space where you can explore movement using your body. This can be a small corner of the room, a wide-open space outdoors, or, if you have access to one, a "dance and movement" space. You can also choose to use music and/or a mirror to practice this creative exercise.

2. **Explore your body's movements.** Without thinking too much, and without judging yourself, begin exploring different body movements, gestures, and postures. Remember the many parts of your body that are capable of showing expression—your hands, fingers, wrists, toes, elbows, hips, knees, head, feet, legs, chest, back, face, etc. Make sure you include facial expressions, too!

3. **Let your body interact with the space.** Play around with different levels in the space. Reach up high, bend over, squat, sit, roll, lie flat, curl into a ball, and jump. Experiment with the multitude of levels your body can have in the space.

4. **Connect your body language to your emotions.** Once you've explored your body's movements and discovered new levels in the space, start to relate your body language to your feelings. What do the different gestures, positions, postures, and movements say?

5. **Reflect.** What stories about yourself are you currently telling, using your body language? What have you discovered in this creative exercise that will help you tell new or different stories with your body?

6. **Go ahead:** *strut your stuff*! Use your new movements to represent yourself in the ways you would like to be seen. Practice walking and talking while using the body language you aspire to. Add a theme song to the movements that will inspire your newly expressive self.

Revisit, repurpose, reinvent

Re-energise your creative practice

Use intentional exploration and imagination spaces to expand the possibilities of an ordinary object. Open up opportunities to repurpose and reinvent your creative energy.

Exercise these creative muscles:

Imagination
Practice stretching your imagination muscles to go beyond conventional thinking and expand your capacity to invent disruptive ideas and concepts.

Reinvention
Exercise your ability to turn existing materials and ideas into new stories and creations.

How to...

1. **Find an object.** It can be anything!
2. **Recognise—then un-recognise.** Take a moment to recognise the object for what you know it to be. What are its main functions? Then erase its usual definition from your mind.
3. **Explore your object.** Use all of your senses to explore the characteristics of your object. Don't forget to listen to the sounds it can make! You can also take your object apart.
4. **List its characteristics.** What did you discover about your object while exploring it? Write down each of the characteristics you noticed. Think about its texture and form. Imagine what might happen to the object if it were crushed, melted, cut into pieces, or torn apart.
5. **Give it context.** Consider how the object could act in different contexts to help launch fresh ways of thinking about it. Don't be afraid to place it in situations or environments where it wouldn't normally be found or used. For example, try placing a soccer ball in an opera house or think about how to use an empty plastic bottle in an orchestra.
6. **Unleash your imagination.** Use the different characteristics of the object to imagine new uses for it. Practice inhabiting new viewpoints. See it through the eyes of a child, the perspective of an animal, or the expectations of a different culture.
7. **Prototype your ideas.** Sketch out the new uses you've come up with, or build them into models.

Sounds like music

Discover the music all around you

Practice opening your eyes and ears to the signs and sounds of inspiration that surround you. Experiment with everyday objects to make noise and create music.

Exercise these creative muscles:

Opening your senses

When you practice active listening, you open up your senses to connect to sources of inspiration surrounding you that you may not otherwise notice.

Experimentation

Practice exploring new ways to do things through sound. Learning to experiment trains you to focus on the creative process and let go of fixating on creative outputs.

How to...

1. **Open your ears.** First, close your eyes and listen closely to the sounds in your environment. Practice this for a few minutes. Connect to the different ways your ears find sounds when you focus on active listening.
2. **Now listen with your eyes.** Open your eyes and look around you. What do the sounds look like now that your eyes are open? Where are the sounds coming from? How are they being made?
3. **Find an instrument.** Locate an object to explore and use as an instrument. It can be anything—be creative! Try some of these suggestions to get started: 1. Choose a recycled item—maybe a tin can, rubber band, or water bottle. 2. Find something in nature, like rocks, sticks, leaves, or water. 3. Use your body—your hands, feet, mouth, or voice.
4. **Make music.** Explore your "instrument". What different sounds can you create? Play with the sounds you hear to make music. Think of different rhythms, tones, and melodies.
5. **Experiment, document, and mix it.** Now that you have different musical sounds, find creative ways of mixing them. Record different tracks using a mobile device. Invite friends to play their instruments. Create music together.

Mono-chromatic masterpieces

Activate body and mind for making

Choose a colour and take a walking "treasure hunt" to find objects in that colour, connecting your body and mind as creative collaborators. Design playful compositions using monochromatic objects to exercise your problem-solving skills.

Exercise these creative muscles:

Making and prototyping

When you use your hands to actively create things, you are exercising your capacity to bring ideas to the making stage so they can live in the real world, outside of your imagination.

Problem-solving

Practice synthesising information by choosing your objects, then solve problems and expand your capacity to make creative decisions through your compositions.

How to...

1. **Set up your canvas.** Think about the approximate size of your composition while in your creative space. You can set up a piece of blank paper or mark out a space on your desk or the floor. Think of this as your "canvas".

2. **Collect objects of the same colour.** Red, yellow, pink, blue... you choose! Decide on a colour, then gather a range of objects representing different shades of the colour you chose, from light to dark.

3. **Be curious and open-minded.** Your objects can be anything! Odd objects, recycled objects, scraps of paper, anything you like. Enjoy choosing different sizes, textures, and forms.

4. **Return to your canvas.** Take your monochromatic collection back to your creative space.

5. **Compose the objects.** Begin arranging your objects to fill your canvas. You can start by placing them in a shape, like a square, rectangle, circle, or triangle.

6. **Play.** Create multiple combinations of objects until your composition feels "right" for you. There are no rules or expectations. It's your process.

7. **Capture your "final" composition.** Once you feel your composition is complete, you can take a photo of it and save it. This way you can try new iterations of your composition. Or, if you love your creation, and it is possible to glue the objects in place, you can make it a more permanent creation.

Library
launch pad

Books as creative prompts

Libraries are filled with creativity! The many authors, researchers, and artists who came before you have given you a creative gift. Each and every word, illustration, or story living inside of the pages of a book offers a chance for you to continue building on their creative energy.

Exercise these creative muscles:

Connecting the dots
The process of discovering fresh connections between small chunks of information exercises your capacity to work more easily with creative constraints or limitations.

Be open
Taking things out of context and finding a new use for them builds the muscles of an open mindset.

How to...

1. **Words.** Take a book, magazine, or newspaper and choose 50 words at random to use as a writing prompt for a new story or poem. Or pull small excerpts from several books to find a theme that will launch your creative thinking.

2. **Images.** Choose an image from an art book, a children's book, or a book on culture to launch your creative process. Make, write, imagine, "copy", dance, reflect... you decide how to use this as inspiration.

3. **Culture.** Explore different ways of life by looking for traditional stories from a particular culture or researching its heritage and customs. What does learning about a new culture inspire in you? How might you incorporate different traditions, images, and stories into your creative work or life?

Continue developing your creative toolbox

Scan the QR code for more ways to kickstart your creativity and keep your momentum going!

Visit me at **www.hollyblondin.com** to say hello.

We are always better creators in collaboration.

Acknowledgements

Thank you to all of my students, past, present, and future. What you teach me at every turn is a gift. This book exists because of *you*.

I am grateful to the institutions and organisations over the years that connected me to beautiful minds and allowed me to share my experience with people daring to *be* creative.

Thanks to my BIS publishing team: Harm van Kessel for believing in me and the work, Soraya Clevers for your zeal and collaboration, Peter Notebaart in production for keeping it real, and the entire team for going to bat for this book to bring it to readers. Thanks also to Bionda Dias, for being the first believer and for making the connection within BIS.

I want to acknowledge the hard work of my talented professional creative team. Without their expertise and creative ideas, we never could have flown!

Editor Gillian Moore is a writer's gift—thank you for making me a better writer by touching this book with your brilliance, page by page, and for your zest and fervour in sharing this journey with me from one creative soul to another.

A special thanks to Nihal Pimpale, whose continuous enthusiasm for my work drove so much of this creative process. Not only did you bring the spirit of this book alive with your book cover design, but your generous design leadership also made this project an unforgettable experience.

I'm grateful to Jessica Saggu, who designed the book's beautiful interior. Your supreme talent elevated my vision! Also, thank you for bringing your calm and positive attitude to the creative struggle so we could birth this baby—yes or yes.

Thank you to proofreader Eliza Ariadni Kalfa for your eagle eyes and literary expertise.

Thanks to web designer Vibeke Foss, *Gorgeous Geek*, for making my wild ideas a reality with your technical magic.

Thanks to Mindy "Helen" Doychich for sharing this process with me from its inception as a trusted sister and friend, and for weaving in your expertise as an educator, helping to take this idea from a creative card deck to this realised dream—a book!

I want to thank my creative genius husband, Didier Lourenço, for creating the space for me to *be* creative, for continuing to ask me the hard questions, and for showing me for decades how to live a successful and satisfying creative life. "*We know.*"

Thank you, Paulina Larocca, for your expertise and guidance in every stage of publishing my first book. Your collaboration on the business aspects of delivering a book enlightened me, and your cleverness in the creative phases helped me to launch. You are First Class Yoghurt!

A special thanks to my family for believing in every creative idea I have ever entertained. Your neverending support fuels me and inspires me to keep going. Thank you in particular to my parents Cheryl Blondin ("Mom"), for always encouraging my writing habits, and Patrick Blondin ("Dad"), for leading with your curiosity. I am grateful to Lindsey Cabrera, for your creativity, and to Martin Cabrera, John Doychich, Sylvie Lourenço, Fulvio Lourenço, and Piedad Lourenço (especially for your candles). Thanks to my late Grandma B. whose sound advice lives on.

Thank you to my tribe of friends and colleagues for engaging in this book's long journey, reading first drafts, offering feedback, and for the constant enthusiasm and support that gave me the courage to tackle this process: Lisa Danser; Susan Hurley for inspiring #SDFF; the Hurley artists Gregg, Keegan, and Nathan; Chelsea C. Hayes; Edward Rogoff; Emma Jean Price; Edward Cardimona; Christoph Winkler; and Deep Parekh.

I also want to express my wider gratitude to all of the inspiring people who have crossed my path in my lifetime (too many to name). So many rich experiences and emotions have taught me to *start from where you are.* Without the highs, the lows, and the important lessons learned along the way, year after year, this process wouldn't have been as rewarding as it is now.

And finally, thank you to those on my creative family tree whose books on creativity, or creative approaches, influenced and inspired me to write this book: Lisa Congdon, Twyla Tharp, Austin Kleon, Elle Luna, Dennis DeSantis, Adam J. Kurtz, Danielle Krysa, and Maurice Sendak.

About the author

Holly Blondin has spent her entire life as a creative practitioner and knows just how real the creative struggle truly is. Over the past 25 years, she has had multiple creative careers, as a musical theatre performing artist with a one-woman cabaret show; an entrepreneur and artist running her own greeting card business; a marketing and branding professional; and a strategic designer teaching at Parsons School of Design. Holly holds a BFA from Western Michigan University and an MBA from Zicklin School of Business, Baruch College New York. Throughout her many creative endeavours, Holly has had the privilege of partnering with extraordinarily talented people to create a unique portfolio of work that is as diverse as her passions. She is dedicated to bridging the gap between creative and business mindsets. Nowadays, when she's not in the classroom or in her studio working on a new project, she runs a thriving creative consultancy and develops innovative workshops for clients worldwide. Her creativity and curiosity first transformed this native Michigander into a New Yorker before leading her to Europe, where she now calls Barcelona home.